APPLIED HINDUISM

Ancient Wisdom for Today's World

APPLIED
HINDUISM
Ancient Wisdom for Today's World

Gyan Rajhans | Subhamoy Das

Indus Source Books

Indian Spirit, Universal Wisdom

Indus Source Books
PO Box 6194
Malabar Hill PO
Mumbai 400 006
INDIA
Email: info@indussource.com
www.indussource.com

Applied Hinduism: Ancient Wisdom for Today's World

First published in India by Indus Source Books in 2018

ISBN: 978-93-85509-24-7

Copyright © Gyan Rajhans & Subhamoy Das, 2018

Cover photographs and design by Ajay Rawat

Inside photographs and illustrations by Subhamoy Das

All rights reserved

Printed at Thomson Press India Ltd., New Delhi.

This book is sold subject to the condition that it shall not by way of trade or otherwise, be lent, resold, hired out, or otherwise circulated without the publisher's prior written consent in any form of binding or cover other than that in which it is published and without a similar condition including this condition being imposed on the subsequent purchaser and without limiting the rights under copyright reserved above, no part of this publication may be reproduced, stored in a retrieval system, or transmitted in any form, or by any means, electronic, mechanical, photocopying, recording or otherwise, without the prior written permission of both the copyright owner and the publisher of this book.

CONTENTS

II. GOODNESS OF THE SCRIPTURES
What we can apply in our everyday life from the teachings of Hindu holy text

III. GODS AS SYMBOLS
What we can learn from the symbolism and iconography of Hindu deities

In the history of the world, Hinduism is the only religion that exhibits a complete independence and freedom of the human mind, its full confidence in its own powers. Hinduism is freedom, especially the freedom in thinking about God.

Dr. Sarvepalli Radhakrishnan
President of India (1962-67)

Preface

The vast wealth of spiritual wisdom that ancient Vedic sages and scholars have left behind can be of immense help in healing the restless minds and bodies of today's generation.

Most of us today find ourselves caught in a web of relentless pursuit of everyday goals. The stress and negative energies produced by the daily toil manifest themselves as maladies of the mind and body.

Spiritual knowledge has the power to bring even the busiest of men and women from the brink of burnout, help them enjoy the fruits of their labor, and assist them in making the choices they need to make at every crossroad in life.

Unfortunately, despite our long heritage of spiritual teachings, many of today's globally aligned people, especially the youth, are disdainful of spiritual pursuits, trashing them as 'unfashionable.' Inwardly, of course, they long for peace and quiet to make sense of the mad race they are in.

This book is not just for seekers of spirituality and peace, it is also for those who want to make sense of the faith they follow mechanically, and make the most of the wisdom that lies buried in our great scriptures.

I
Back to Basics

What makes up the building blocks of
Sanatana Dharma and Vedic tradition

Making Sense of Sanatana Dharma

Sanatana Dharma, or what is known as 'Hinduism' today, originally means 'eternal duty.' This duty is shared by all living beings and also includes moral codes of conduct, and religious laws and principles.

Hinduism lacks a unified system of beliefs and ideas. It represents a broad spectrum of beliefs and practices, which are on one hand akin to paganism, pantheism and the like, and on the other hand similar to profound, abstract and metaphysical ideas.

There is no one kind of Hinduism. Hinduism is a conglomerate of diverse beliefs and traditions. The prominent themes of Hinduism include:

- *Dharma* (ethics and duties)
- *Samsara* (rebirth)
- *Karma* (right action)
- *Moksha* (liberation from the cycle of *samsara*)

Moral ideals in Hinduism include non-violence, truthfulness, friendship, compassion, fortitude, self-control, purity, and generosity.

Since religion and culture are nearly interchangeable terms in Hinduism, emotive expressions such as *bhakti* (devotion), or *dharma* (what is right), and *yoga* (discipline) are used to depict the essential aspects of the religion.

Human life is divided into four stages, and there are defined rites and rituals for each stage—from birth till death.

Traditional Hinduism has two life-long *dharmas* that one can follow: *grihastha dharma* (domestic religion), and *sannyasin dharma* (ascetic religion). *Grihastha dharma* has four goals: *kāma* (sensual pleasure), *artha* (wealth and prosperity), *dharma* (the laws of life), and *moksha* (liberation from the cycle of births). The *sannyasin dharma* recognizes *moksha* as its ultimate goal.

The basic scriptures of Hinduism, which is collectively referred to as *Shastras*, are essentially a collection of spiritual laws propounded by various saints and sages at different points in its long history. The two types of sacred writings comprise the Hindu scriptures: *Shruti* (heard), and *Smriti* (memorized). They were passed orally from generation to generation for centuries before they were written down, mostly in the Sanskrit language. The major and most popular Hindu texts include the *Bhagavad Gita*, the *Upanishads*, and the epics of *Ramayana* and *Mahabharata*.

Hinduism believes that there is only one supreme Absolute called the *Brahman*. However, it does not advocate the worship of any one particular deity. There are thousands and even millions of gods and goddesses in the Hindu pantheon, each representing some aspects of the *Brahman*. Therefore, the Hinduism faith is characterized by the multiplicity of deities. The most fundamental of Hindu deities is the trinity of Brahma, Vishnu, and Shiva—the creator, the preserver, and the destroyer, respectively. Hindus also worship spirits, trees, animals, and even planets.

The Five Principles and Ten Disciplines

What are the main principles of the Hindu way of life? And what are the ten commandments of the Sanatana Dharma? Here are 15 easy-to-remember tenets of Hinduism:

Five Principles

1. God exists: There is one absoluteOm. There is one trinity of Brahma, Vishnu, and Maheshwara (Shiva). There are several divine forms.
2. All human beings are divine
3. Unity of existence through love
4. Religious harmony
5. Knowledge of three Gs: Ganga (sacred river), Gita (sacred script), and Gayatri (sacred mantra)

Ten Disciplines

1. *Satya* (truth)

2. *Ahimsa* (non-violence)
3. *Brahmacharya* (celibacy, non-adultery)
4. *Asteya* (no desire to possess or steal)
5. Aparighara (non-corrupt)
6. *Shaucha* (cleanliness)
7. *Santosh* (contentment)
8. *Swadhyaya* (reading of scriptures)
9. *Tapas* (austerity, perseverance, penance)
10. *Ishwarpranidhan* (regular prayers)

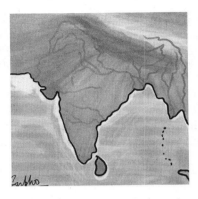

The Genesis of Hinduism

Unlike other religions of the world, Hinduism, or more correctly Sanatana Dharma, neither originated from a single founder or scripture nor began at a particular point in time. It is impossible to define the exact time and place of its origin. An approximate date of 2000 BCE (Before Common Era, i.e., before the year zero in terms of the Gregorian calendar) is usually quoted to be the origin of Hinduism in the standard Western textbooks. This date is based on the old Aryan Invasion Theory, which has now been completely discredited. According to this theory, the Vedic Aryans came from central Asia, invaded India around 2000 BCE, destroyed the more advanced indigenous Harappan civilization and established the Vedic culture. Based on the current archeological and literary evidence, modern scholars have concluded that there never was an Aryan invasion, and that the Vedic people who called themselves Aryans were indigenous to India, being one of the original ethnic groups since 6500 BCE or even earlier.

The word 'Arya' in Sanskrit means wise and noble. It is a word of honorable address, and not a racial reference coined by European scholars and put to its perverse use by the Nazis. There is now evidence that Hinduism must have existed even around 10,000 BCE.

The first vernal equinox recorded in the Rig Veda is now known to have occurred in 10,000 BCE.

The Oldest Surviving Religion

Nobody knows when Hinduism or Sanatana Dharma was

born. However, it's a well-established fact that Hinduism is the oldest surviving religion in the world. Ancient sages and rishis sang divine songs in the forests and on the riverbanks of India thousands of years before Moses, Buddha, or Christ walked the Earth. Sanatana Dharma thus flourished from the prehistoric times in India in the form of a monotheistic Hindu pantheon—the worship of one Supreme Lord in various ways and forms.

However, unlike the origin of Hinduism, there is general consensus among scholars about the term 'Hindu'. The agreement is that, as early as 500 BCE, the ancient Persians called the Indian people living on the banks of the River Indus the 'Sindhus.' In the Persian language, the letter 'S' is pronounced as the letter 'H.' Hence, the word 'Sindhu' became 'Hindu.' The people living in India came to be known as the Hindus, irrespective of what religion they followed.

There is another theory about the origin of the word Hinduism. According to Sadhguru Jaggi Vasudev, the word 'Hindu' is a geographical identity as it owes its name to the mountains and seas surrounding the Indian peninsula. 'Hi' comes from the 'Himalayas' and 'indu' from 'Indu Sagara,' the ancient name of the Indian Ocean. He goes on to say that because of these two geographical features, India enjoyed an undisturbed civilization that thrived over many millennia, resulting in the flowering of the human genius in many forms—from art and culture to science and technology, and all the wisdom of India that we are so proud of today.

A Historical Timeline

This broad timeline of the history of Hinduism will give you an idea about the major events that shaped the world's oldest extant faith.

6500 or prior to 2000 BCE: This is the period in which the hymns of Rig Veda (the oldest Hindu scriptures) were developed.

1500 to 500 BCE: This is the period in which the Upanishads were composed. Buddhism and Jainism developed during this period. The Mahabharata and Ramayana were also enhanced during this period. The two epics were composed much earlier, though no one knows exactly when (possibly 2000 BCE or earlier). The *Bhagavad Gita* is part of the Mahabharata. The laws of Manu or the Hindu code of conduct were also written during this time.

AD 300 to 1500: This is the period in which the Puranic and Tantric literature were developed.

AD 750 to 1000: This is considered the period of establishment of Shankara's Advaita Vedanta philosophy and the decline of Buddhism in India.

AD 1000-1800: This is the period that experienced the rise of devotional worship expounded by the Alwars, Nayanars, Tulsidas, Surdas, Tukaram, Ramprasad, Ramanuja, Ramanand, Gurunanak, Meerabai, Vallavacharya, Chaitanaye Mahaprabhu, and many other religious teachers and saints.

Modern Hindu Renaissance

History has not been kind to the Hindus and their religion in India. A long and brutal spell of foreign domination and the religious fervor of foreign missionaries posed numerous challenges to the survival of Hinduism in the country. At the same time, India had the good fortune of producing a number of illustrious religious and spiritual leaders who revolutionized Hinduism by opposing certain inhumane social practices, including the vices of the caste system and excess ritualism. The leaders of the modern Hindu renaissance include Raja Ram Mohan Roy, Swami Dayanand Saraswati, Paramhans Ramakrishna, Swami Vivekananda, Sri Aurobindo, Ramana Maharishi, and Mahatma Gandhi.

The insights of Hindu Dharma spread to other parts of the world through emissaries who visited India and from Indians who visited foreign lands. A key proponent of this movement to the Western world was Swami Vivekananda. He was a popular speaker at the World Parliament of Religions held in Chicago in September 1893. Later, Paramhansa Yoganand, the author of *Autobiography of a Yogi,* came to the United States in 1920 and helped spread the universal ideals of Sanatana Dharma. He established the Self-Realization Fellowship in California to disseminate Vedic teachings.

There are many more prominent figures who have spread significant Hindu spirituality in the Western world such as Swami Rama Tirtha, Swami Ramdas, Swami Sivananada, Sri Satya Sai Baba, Maa Anand Mai, Swami A.C. Bhaktivedanta, Maharishi Mahesh Yogi, Swami Chinmayananda, Satguru Subramuniyaswami, Sadhguru Jaggi Vasudev, and Mata Amritanandamayi.

Dharma Versus Religion

Religion literally means that which leads one to God. *Dharma* is derived from the root Sanskrit word *dhri*, which means 'to hold together'. It has a wider meaning than the word 'religion'. There is no equivalent word for *dharma* in English or any other language. *Dharma* does not mean religion; it is the law that governs all action. In this sense, Hinduism is not a religion; it's a *dharma*. For centuries, the world has misinterpreted this. Out of this misinterpretation have emerged many misconceptions about Hinduism as a religion, which essentially is the Hindu Dharma.

Dharma is the moral law combined with spiritual discipline that guides one's life. The Hindus consider *dharma* the very foundation of life. The Atharva Veda describes *dharma* symbolically, *Prithivim dharmana dhritam*—this world is upheld by *dharma*.

Dharma is the path of righteousness and living one's life according to the codes of conduct described by the Vedas and Upanishads. *Dharma* means 'that which holds the people of this world and the whole creation'. It refers to the religious ethics propounded by Hindu gurus in ancient Indian scriptures. Tulsidas, the author of *Ramcharitmanas*, has defined the root of *dharma* as 'compassion.' This principle was taken up by Lord Buddha in his immortal book of great wisdom *Dhammapada*.

Dharma is like a cosmic norm, and if one goes against the norm it can result in bad *karma*. So, *dharma* affects the future according to the *karma* accumulated. Therefore, one's *dharmic* path in the next life is necessary to bring to fruition all the results of past *karma*.

The term *dharma* can best be explained as the 'law of being' without which things cannot exist, just as the essential factor in a human being is life or the *atman* without which he or she cannot exist. Therefore, the *dharma* of a human being is the *atman*. Hence, any good *atmic* quality is *dharmic*. *Dharma* therefore implies duty or a course of conduct. For example, Hinduism endorses the idea that it is one's *dharma* to marry, raise a family and provide for that family in whatever way it is necessary.

Those who profess the Hindu Dharma and seek to follow it are guided by spiritual, social and moral rules, actions, knowledge and duties, which are responsible for holding the human race together.

The Hindu Dharma is also known by the names Sanatana Dharma and Vaidik Dharma. *Sanatana* means eternal and all-pervading and *vaidik* means based on the Vedas.

In simple terms, one can say that dharma means a code of conduct, i.e. doing the right thing, in thought, word and deed, bearing in mind always that the Supreme Being is behind all our deeds. This is the teaching of the Vedas, which are the original source of Hindu Dharma. *Vedo - Khilo Dharma Moolam.*

According to Swami Sivananda, "Hinduism allows absolute freedom to the rational mind of man. It never demands any undue restraint upon the freedom of human reason, the freedom of thought, feeling and will of man. Hinduism is a religion of freedom, allowing the widest margin of freedom in matters of faith and worship. It allows absolute freedom of human reason and heart with regard to questions as the nature of God, soul, form of worship, creation, and the goal of life. It does not force anybody to accept particular dogmas or forms of worship. It allows everybody to reflect, investigate, enquire and cogitate."

Hence, all manners of religious faiths, various forms of worship or spiritual practices, diverse rituals and customs have found their place, side by side, within the Hindu Dharma. They have been cultured and developed in harmony with one another. The Hindu Dharma, unlike other religions, does not dogmatically assert that the final emancipation or liberation is possible only through its means and not through any other. The Hindu Dharma is only one kind of mean to an end. All means ultimately lead to the final goal that has been approved of.

The religious hospitality of the Hindu Dharma is proverbial. The Hindu Dharma is extremely liberal and catholic. This is its fundamental feature. It pays respect to all religions and does not revile any religion. It accepts and honors truth from wherever it comes, in whatever garb it is presented.

Yato dharmah tato jayah – Where *dharma* exists, victory is guaranteed.

What's the Deal About Karma?

India must be credited for giving the world the most profound, rational and scientific answer to several of man's questions: Why are some people born poor and why are some rich? Can we do something wrong and get away with it? Why should we be good to our parents, neighbors, friends, society and country? Why should we not be selfish? Only the karma theory explains these questions in a logical manner.

The word 'karma' comes from the root 'kr,' which means 'action,' 'doing' or 'acting.' In philosophic and spiritual thought, the doctrine of karma has come to mean 'cause and effect' and 'action and reaction' to which all human conduct is subjected to.

The Gita says, "No creature remains even for a moment without being engaged in karma. Thus, all the actions that a man performs, e.g., breathing, eating, drinking, sleeping, desiring, are included in karma."

Newton's Third Law

Like Newton's third law of motion, every karma or action has a reaction, which is equal and opposite. In other words, every cause results in an effect and in turn the effect becomes a further cause, resulting in a further effect and so on. As no cause remains without its due effect and a like action produces a like result, the doctrine of karma is that unseen law that adjusts itself wisely, intelligently and equitably, and each effect has its cause, tracing the latter back to its producer.

Effects of Karma

Although the mind-created karma acts on the mental and

physical planes, its effect takes place in the following three ways.

1. Any action boomerangs on the doer: A harmful action done to another person eventually harms the perpetrator.
2. The action reflects in retribution: A man eating more than his share may die of a weak stomach.
3. The action acts in a symbolic way. A man killing an innocent creature may be infected with a wasting disease like anemia.

Karma may have been done in the immediate past or the remote past. We may or may not remember it. It survives in the form of a seed with us and manifests at the appropriate time.

In the Mahabharata, it is said, "Karma follows man like his shadow. It sits with him while he sits, moves with him while he moves. It works on him even when he is working. Just as fruits and flowers come to the trees at the appointed time, not impelled by any one, one's past or karma never transgresses its appointed time."

The reaction to good or bad karma seldom begins immediately. It takes time for the karmic seed to sprout and come to fruition. How and when are not known, but it is a fact that no one can escape from his karma. The Lord Buddha has said, "Not in the sky, not in the midst of the sea, not if we enter into the clefts of the mountain, is there known a spot in the whole world where a man might be freed from his deeds."

Birth to Rebirth

Now the obvious question is does karma pass on from birth to rebirth, and if it does, are we free to change the effect of past life karma in this life? The answer, according to Hindu scriptures, is that what we did in the past life remains latent and continues with us, manifesting itself at the appropriate time. For example, if you did an act of kindness just before you died, it will be returned to you as an act of kindness in your next life. An act of cruelty will come back to you as an act of cruelty. Karma is the cause of the cycle of births. You may call it the rebirth latent.

Freedom of Action and Karma

On freedom of action and karma, Dr. Radhakrishnan has said, "They are two aspects of the same reality. We are all the time making our own karma and thus determining the character of our next birth." As Pascal puts it, "Though we are slaves of the past, we are master of the future."

We can say, karma accumulated in the present life can modify the karma inherited from our past lives. It is a simple arithmetic of debit and credit. If you have acquired sufficient credit by doing good Karma, it may wipe out the effect of bad deeds—the debit you were born with.

Thus, knowledge of the doctrine of karma destroys the cause of hate, envy and jealousy and the ill-will we may have for our neighbor, friend or any other fellow being. It makes us realize that we are punished by our bad deeds and not for them. It removes impatience from our mind and places infinite time before us for our evolution. It makes us realize that no effort of ours is ever wasted and at every stage we are surpassing ourselves and not the others.

This is a very short treatise in the doctrine of Karma because, as the Gita says, "*Gahana karmano gatih*" (Gita 4:17) (the effects of karma are unfathomable)."

Are Hindus Idol Worshipers?

No. Hindus are not idol worshipers in the sense implied by the dictionary, which defines 'idol' as a false god or a form or appearance visible but without substance. A sacred image used in Hindu worship represents a particular manifestation of the ultimate reality of the *Brahman*. The substance that the sacred image represents is the ultimate reality and none other. Thus, the Hindus' worship of the sacred images of God is neither a false god nor is it without any substance. How can then image worship be called idol worship in the sense implied by Webster's dictionary? The image itself is not God, but a symbol of God. The Hindus do not worship the image as God but they worship God through an image. To worship an image as God is idolatry, but to worship God through an image is a valid form of worship.

Symbolic Form of God

In every religion, God is worshiped in some form. Christians worship the crucifix as a symbol of Christ, and Muslims adore Kaaba in Mecca as the most sacred symbol of God. Other examples are the Adi Granth Shrine in the Golden Temple of Amritsar, the Arc and Tora of the Jews, the image of the meditating Buddha, the totems of indigenous faiths, and the artifacts of many holy men of all religions. There are several such allegorical examples. But the bottom line is that in every religion, God is worshiped in some form, and Hinduism admits it openly.

It is interesting to note that when sacred images are used in other religions, they are called icons and regarded as holy works of art. But when sacred images are used by the Hindus, they are called 'idols'. In the words of Dr David Frawley, an American Vedic scholar, "An image of Christ as the good shepherd is called an icon and viewed with respect. An image of Krishna as the good cow herder, which is similar to the image of the Divine, watching over the souls of men, is called an idol, which encourages one to look down on it. This is prejudice and negative stereotyping in the language of the worst order."

Why Are There So Many Images?

Now one may say they can understand the symbolic meaning of image worship by Hindus, but he or she may question why there are so many forms. Are they not very confusing? Yes, it is confusing, if one doesn't understand the following logic.

First of all, the Hindu religion recognizes the diversity of the human mind and the potential for a different level of spiritual development in each individual. The religion does not shove everyone into the pigeonhole of a single creed. The Hindu scriptures declare, "*Aakashad pathitham thoyam yatha gacchathi sagaram. Sarva deva namaskaraha Keshavam prati gacchathi.*" This means just as the rainwater that falls from the sky eventually reaches the ocean, so does all the worship offered to Him (that is God / *Brahman*)—by whatever name you wish to call Him or whatever form you like. Everything ultimately goes to the one and only ultimate Infinite Supreme Reality.

Secondly, being the creator of innumerable forms in this universe, the Supreme Being is able to assume any form to please his devotees. Furthermore, the Supreme Being cannot be said to have only one particular form or name, as that would imply putting limitations on his infinite power. That is why the Hindus worship various names and forms of the Supreme Reality.

No Superior or Inferior Form

No name or form is considered superior or inferior to others, because all of them are various manifestations of one Supreme Being. When a devotee chooses to worship one form or one image of the Supreme Being, the chosen deity is called *isht dev* or *isht devata*. This personal *isht dev* becomes the object of the devotee's love and adoration and satisfies his spiritual longing.

There is another thing about the Hindu philosophy of image worship. When an idol of a deity is carved and packed, shipped and unpacked, and kept inside a temple, it is still not ready for worship. Worship starts when a ritual is performed to invoke the physical presence of the deity into the stone image. This ritual is called *pran pratishtha*, which literally means 'making the image a sacred medium to help devotees offer their devotion to God.'

Symbols We Live By

A symbol is a conventional sign employed to convey a meaning. In various religions, God is depicted using various symbols. The use of symbols greatly helps us understand the Infinite Almighty God. One needs a clear, unbiased mind to comprehend the truth behind symbols. An organized study of symbols takes us to another concept—that of symbolism. Symbolism is the representation of something moral or spiritual by something natural or material.

In Hinduism, symbols have been used from time immemorial. Most of the symbols of Hinduism are derived from the Vedas. Symbolism is an important way in Hinduism for the realization of divine knowledge. But the science of symbolism has not been laid down clearly and openly based on principles in any of the Hindu scriptures. It must be studied patiently, devotedly and humbly.

The degree and the manner in which this science has been imparted and understood are varied, depending upon the capacity of those who have received it. There are many opinions and explanations of symbols. Even popular idols and images vary on the point of detail. Let's look at a detailed interpretation of three major symbols used in Hinduism.

Om or Aum

Om or *Aum* is of paramount importance in Hinduism. This syllable represents the *Brahman* and the unmanifest aspects of God; it is called *pranav,* which means that which pervades life through our *prana* or breath.

The symbol of *Om* or *Aum* consists of three curves, one semicircle and a dot. The large lower curve symbolizes the waking state. In this state, the consciousness is turned outwards through the gates of the senses. The large size signifies that this is the most common (majority) state of the human consciousness.

The upper curve denotes the state of deep sleep or unconscious state. This is a state where the sleeper neither desires something nor beholds any dream.

The middle curve signifies the dream state. In this state, the consciousness of the individual is turned inwards, and that is the reason for this curve pointing towards the other two curves.

These are the three states of an individual's consciousness. As the Hindu mystic thought believes that the entire manifested reality springs from this consciousness, these three curves represent the entire physical phenomenon.

The dot signifies the fourth state of consciousness, known in Sanskrit as *turiya*. In this state, the consciousness looks neither outwards nor inwards nor the two states together. It signifies the coming to rest of all differentiated and relative existence. This utterly quiet, peaceful and blissful state is the ultimate aim of all spiritual activity. This absolute (non-relative) state illuminates the other three states.

Finally, the semicircle symbolizes *maya* (cosmic illusion) and separates the dot from the other three curves. It is the illusion of *maya* that prevents us from the realization of the highest state of bliss.

The semicircle is open at the top. When ideally drawn, it does not touch the dot. This means this highest state is not affected by *maya*. *Maya* only affects the manifested phenomenon. This effect prevents the seeker from reaching his ultimate goal, the realization of the one, all-pervading, and absolute principle. In this manner, the geometric shape of Om represents both the unmanifest and the manifest aspects.

The Swastika

It is a symbol of auspicious knowledge. The term *swastika* emanates from the Sanskrit word *swasti* where *su* is good and *asti* is being.

The *swastika is* a line design invented by the Vedic sages. Its geometry is believed to have some relation with certain natural energy fields. It is drawn as a cross with equal arms, when all the arms are continued as far again at right angles clockwise.

The symbol of *swastika* has been used as a holy sign in India since the time of yore. Scriptural descriptions define it as a divine symbol that encompasses, in coded form, several important meanings, mysterious formulae and signs representing specific energy cycles in the universe. In some scriptures, four divine powers governing the physical system of nature are said to be subtly present around its four sides. Scholars of Vedic literature also interpret the *swastika* symbol as the coded design of the electromagnetic / magnetic energy fields around the solar system's nucleus.

The Poorna Kumbha

Poorna kumbha literally means a 'full pitcher' where *poorna* means full and *kumbha* is a pot. The *poorna kumbha* is decorated with the *swastika* design and consists of water, fresh mango or betel leaves, and a coconut on top. It is generally placed as the chief deity or by the side of the deity before starting a *puja* (Hindu worship). The pot symbolizes Mother Earth, the water symbolizes the life-giver, the leaves symbolize life, and the coconut symbolizes divine consciousness. Commonly used during most religious rites, the pitcher with the *swastika* on it also stands for auspiciousness and harbinger of good fortune.

These three symbols are universal symbols widely used in Hinduism. In addition to these, every Hindu God and Goddess has many characteristics like the dress, vehicle or *vahana* and weapons, which are themselves symbols of the deity's power. For example, *Brahma* holds the Vedas in his hands; this signifies that he has supreme command over creative and religious knowledge. *Vishnu* holds a conch, which stands for the five elements and eternity; a discus, which is the symbol of the mind; a bow that symbolizes power, and a lotus, which is the symbol of the cosmos. *Shiva's* trident represents the three *gunas* or qualities inherent in human beings. Similarly, Krishna's flute symbolizes divine music, and so on.

To sum up, a symbol in Hinduism is the objective representation of a subjective idea.

The Basis of Caste System

If we were to state that the caste system has nothing to do with Sanatana Dharma or the Hindu religion as such, we would be evading the most corrupt and socially exploitable issue in Hinduism. Today, everyone, whether he or she is a Hindu or a non-Hindu, knows that the caste system is nothing but a degenerated version of the old guild system whereby the son took up the father's profession; this eliminates competition and accounts for a lot of undeserved and frivolous lethargy and nepotism. It is indeed a fact that, with the passage of time, like all other institutions, the original concept of the *varna* system, explained below, became corrupt and birth became the determining factor for establishing one's caste. Gradually, the caste system became a handmade form of social exploitation in Hindu society.

The Origin of the Caste System in Hinduism

When the Vedas refer to the four-fold division of society, they use the Sanskrit word *varna*, meaning class, and not the word *jaati*, which means caste. The word *varna* was mistakenly translated as 'caste' by the Portuguese during their period of colonial establishment in India. In the *varna* system, the creative thinkers and educators were known as Brahmins, not to be confused with the word *Brahman*. The politicians and warriors were known as Kshatriyas; the businessmen, employers and skilled laborers were the Vaishayas, and the non-skilled laborers were the Shudras.

The *varna* system classified an individual into one of these four classes, based upon his or her aptitude, ability, character and achievements as explained by Lord Krishna in the thirteenth shloka of the fourth chapter of the Gita. He says, "The four-fold classification of human beings was created by me in accordance with qualities and actions." The eighteenth chapter of the Gita further expounds the natural classification of individuals, the quality of work performed by them, the knowledge acquired by them, the quality of their wisdom and steadiness, and the concepts of pleasure.

How Castes Are Determined by Qualities

In the Mahabharata, Yudhisthira defines a Brahmin as one who is truthful, forgiving and kind. He clearly points out that a Brahmin is not a Brahmin just because he is born in a Brahmin family; a Shudra is not one because his parents are Shudras.

In one of the most interesting stories in the *Chandogya Upanishad*, a young boy called Satyakama asks his mother, "I wish to receive religious instruction; tell me of what family am I." The mother replies, "I do not know my son. I was a servant in my young age, moving from house to house when I conceived you. I do not know of what family you are. I am Jabala, and you are Satyakama. Say that you are Satykama Jabala."

Satyakama went to Sage Gautam and said to him, "Sir, I wish to receive religious instruction from you. Would you accept me as your student?" The sage asked, "Of what family are you?" Satyakama replied, "I do not know sir. In her young age, my mother went from house to house as a servant and conceived me. She does not know of what family I am. My mother is Jabala and I am Satyakama. Therefore, I am Satyakama Jabala." The sage replied, "No one other than a true Brahmin would speak the truth like this, I will initiate you." This shows that the practice of the *varna* system was based on conduct and character and not on birth.

There are more examples to show that the *varna* system of the Vedas was based upon one's aptitude and natural abilities and not on the hereditary caste structure.

Sage Vyasa, a Brahmin sage and the most revered author of major Hindu scriptures, was the son of Satyawati, a fisherwoman. Vyasa's father, Sage Parasar, had fallen in love with Satyawati at first sight. Vyasa's deep knowledge of the Vedas later determined his caste as a Brahmin sage and not his birth to a fisherwoman.

Sage Valmiki, the celebrated author of the epic Ramayana, was a hunter. He came to be known as a Brahmin sage on the basis of his profound knowledge of the scriptures and his authorship of the Ramayana.

Sage Vidura, the Brahmin sage who gave religious instruction to King Dhritrashtra, was born to a woman servant of the palace. His caste as a Brahmin sage was determined on the basis of his wisdom and knowledge of the *dharma shastras* and scriptures.

Last, but not the least, many consider Mahatma Gandhi, who was by birth a Vaishya, as Brahmin by virtue of his karma.

The Untouchables

Though the division of society based on qualities, actions, and profession was a good idea, in course of time it degenerated. Some say that a fifth division of people emerged in Hindu society and these people were known as 'outcasts' or 'untouchables'. Another group of historians says it was the Shudras who became the untouchables in society. Mahatma Gandhi called the untouchables 'Harijan' (children of God) and fought for their emancipation.

Apart from Mahatma Gandhi, many distinguished people like Raja Ram Mohan Roy and Dr. Sarvepalli Radhakrishanan have relentlessly struggled to get rid of the crude flaws and maladies plaguing Hindu rituals and practices, like caste and untouchability. Maharishi Devendranath Tagore and Keshav Chandra Sen, who founded the Brahmo Somaj; Paramahans Shri Ramakrishna and Swami Vivekananda who established the Ram Krishna Math and Mission; and Swami Dayanand Saraswati, the founder of the Arya Samaj are the other people who were engaged in the process of purifying and revitalizing Hinduism as a way of life.

Casteism is Not Hinduism

The caste system could not have been part of Hindu religious philosophy as it violates the fundamental Hindu doctrine, according to which there is no distinction between individuals as the supreme *Brahman* dwells in the hearts of all beings. Thus, there is no legitimate sanction to the concept of the caste system in the Hindu religion.

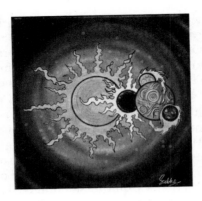

The Story of Creation: From Brahman to Big Bang

Scientists estimate the universe to be ten billion to twenty billion years old. American astrophysicist, Dr Carl Sagan, said, "A millennium before Europeans were willing to divest themselves of the Biblical idea that the world was a few thousand years old, the Hindus were thinking of billions. He further said, "The Hindu religion is the only one of the world's great faiths dedicated to the idea that the cosmos itself undergoes an immense infinite number of deaths and rebirths. It is the only religion where the time scales correspond to those of modern scientific cosmology."

There are quite a few differences in the concepts of creation put forth in the Vedas and the Puranas. Although the explanations about the origin of the universe vary, their conclusions about creation converge.

The Concepts of Genesis

The Hindus believe that the universe is without a beginning (*anadi*) and an end (*anant*). It is the inherent nature of the universe to evolve, devolve and revolve eternally in the cycles of creation, dissolution and recreation. Thus, in Hinduism, there is no such thing as initial creation; creation is eternal and proceeds in cycles. Whenever the words 'beginning' and 'end' are used in Hindu scriptures, they simply mean the beginning and end of a particular cycle.

According to *Manu Smriti*, each cycle of creation is divided into four *yugas* or ages / eras: *Satyuga* (the golden age), *Tretayuga* (silver age), *Dwaparyuga* (copper age) and *Kaliyuga* (iron age). Each cycle of creation begins with *Satyuga*, evolves through *Tretayuga* and *Dwaparyuga*, and ends with the *Kaliyuga*. *Satyuga* is the age of bliss and virtue, as the human intellect is very powerful and able to grasp and obey the spiritual laws underlying the operation of the universe. The spiritual knowledge diminishes and universal chaos increases as the creation evolves from *Satyuga* to *Kaliyuga*.

The total duration of one cycle of the four *yugas* is 12,000 divine years or 4.32 million human years. It is called the *Mahayuga*. One thousand *Mahayugas* comprise one *Kalpa*. At the end of one *Kalpa*, the universe is dissolved by *Pralaya* or cosmic dissolution. It must be noted that this annihilation at the end of *Kalpa* is not a permanent destruction. Cosmic dissolution is a link between the end of one *Kalpa* and the beginning of the next one, in an endless process of cyclic creation. We are currently in the *Kaliyuga*, which began around 3100 BCE. The Hindu notion of time is cyclic and is different from the Western notion of time, which is unidirectional—implying a one-time beginning.

The Vedas on Creation

The *Yajurveda* says that all threads come off the spider, as little sparks come out of the fire. So all the senses, worlds, gods and beings are issued from the self. It says, "This universe is a tree eternally existing, its root aloft and its branches spread below. The pure root of the tree is *Brahman*, the immortal in whom the three worlds have there being, whom none can transcend, who is verily the self." According to the *Yajurveda*, "May God, who in the mystery of His vision and power transforms His white radiance in many colored creations, from whom all things come and into whom all return, grant us the grace of pure vision. Brahman is without beginning, beyond time and space, from whom sprang the three worlds."

The Upanishads and the Cycle of Creation

The metaphysical treatises of the Upanishads predominantly deal with humanity in relation to the universe. The words of Adi Shankara sum up the entire teachings of the Upanishads: "*Brahman* is the reality, the world is unreal... Unreal means anything which is not eternal but is transient, which has a limited life—long or short."

In the Upanishads, the story of the cycle of creation closely resembles that which is described by the modern scientists. The *Mundaka Upanishad* says, "In the beginning, there was *Brahman* and nothing else. There was no matter or energy, no space or time, and no natural laws. *Brahman* was *nirgun* or without any attributes. So, it could not be perceived. *Brahman* expanded, and matter and food were born. From matter arose life and mind, the five elements and the world. All these got into a state of intense activity and change. The result was the universe." Then *Brahman* retired to his dormant self. This is called *Sarga* or primary creation. *Sarga* was followed by *Visarga* or secondary creation, and then evolution carries on.

Since the *Brahman* pervades everything and its creative powers come into play as changes follow one another, new names and forms emerge. Then, at some stage, under the same set of laws, the dissolution of the universe takes place. Matter and energy, space and time, and all the elements of life merge again with the *Brahman*. This whole cycle is called *Kalpa*. In due course, *Kalpa* follows *Kalpa* and everything repeats itself.

The Vedanta philosophy says, "The universe exists in an endless cycle of creation, preservation and destruction. There is neither an absolute end to the world nor is there a duality of God and world, but a unity." This is very much in conformity with modern science that believes in the pulsating universe theory and the Big Bang theory of creation.

Of Heaven and Hell

There are two perspectives on heaven and hell. One point of view is that there is no such place as hell or heaven where you go after death. Both heaven and hell are on earth when you are living. Based on your past karma, you create your own hell and heaven during this life. If you are leading a miserable life, you are in hell. If you have all the amenities of life and have achieved inner peace, you are in heaven.

Another point of view refers to the Vedas, Upanishads, Gita and Puranas and suggests that heaven or hell is situated somewhere up there. The King of the gods, Indra, reigns in heaven and the Lord of Death, Yama, rules hell.

What's Heaven Like?

Swami Shivananda described heaven based on the Puranas: "The heaven of the Hindus is a place where the departed souls go to reap the fruits of their virtuous deeds. They remain there for some time till the fruits of their virtuous actions are exhausted. Then they come back to this world. They eat in heaven the divine feasts of the Shining Ones or the Devas. They move in celestial cars. Indra is the Lord of Heaven or Svarga. Various kinds of Devas (gods) dwell here. Celestial damsels like Urvasi and Rambha dance here. The Gandharvas sing here. There is no disease here. There is no hunger and thirst. The inhabitants are endowed with a brilliant subtle body. They are adorned with shining garments. Heaven is a thought world, a realm of intense ideation. Whatever one wishes, he gets it at once, by immediate materialization. So, it is a happier world than the Earth plane."

What's Hell Like?

Again based on the Puranas and other Hindu Scriptures, Swami Shivananda says: "Hindu Puranas have been very clear on the question of heaven and hell. Writers of law books or *smritis*, like Yajnavalkya and Vishnu, have given a serious description of different kinds of hell and the various pleasures in heaven." Yogi Yajnavalkya mentions twenty-one hells in his law book— they include Raurava, Kumbhipaka, Maharaurava, Tamisra, and Andha Tamisra. The author of *Vishnu Smriti* has also written the same thing.

Hell is a region of sharp, severe and intense pain. The evil doers suffer for a period of time. Bad action is punished and evil doers come back to the Earth plane. They get another chance.

Here's a traditional picture of Hell: The ruler of Hell, Lord Yama, is assisted by Chitragupta. Hell is walled off from the surrounding regions of space by the messengers of Yama. Sinners get a thick body called *Yatana Deha* when they are punished. The punishment in hell is not remembered by the soul when it is reborn. The punishment is reformatory and educative. The permanent educative effect remains in the conscience of the sinner. The innate fear, which some souls feel at the sight of temptation of sin, is due to the finer development of the conscience in the furnace of hell-fire. This is the permanent gain acquired by the soul. The soul is reborn with a keener conscience after being purified by the hell-fire. The sinner can make better use of his faculties in the next birth.

Attainment of Heaven and Hell

Although the above descriptions of heaven and hell resemble the descriptions in Western religions, there is one fundamental difference. The Hindu heaven or hell is not a final dwelling place for an individual soul as stated in the Western religions. After the term of good or bad deeds are over, even the most pious or the most evil person is turned out of heaven or hell as the case may be, to participate once again in the cycle of reincarnation until he or she reaches *moksha* or liberation from the endless chain of deaths and rebirths.

Although several Hindu scriptures refer to the gateways to heaven and hell through good and bad deeds, the *Bhagavad Gita* (6:41) says:

"The unsuccessful yogi, after many, many years of enjoyment on the planets of the pious living entities, is born into a family of righteous people or into a family of rich aristocracy."

In the above *shloka*, 'the planets of pious living entities' means heaven where the doers of meritorious deeds go. But this heaven is not eternal. When the merit capital of the person is exhausted, he or she comes back to the human world, reborn in a pure and prosperous family. Thus, he or she starts life's journey once again, wherever he or she had left off. Nothing of what he or she has done is lost.

The Gita further says, "When one dies in the mode of goodness, he attains the pure higher planets of the great sages." This *shloka* implies that there are different kinds of planets for different kinds of living entities. Those who die in the mode of goodness are elevated to the planets where great sages and great devotees live.

The Gita also mentions: "There are three gates leading to hell—lust, anger and greed. Every sane man should give these up, for they lead to the degradation of the soul." This *shloka* says that if a man or woman wants to avoid hell, he or she must try to give up lust, anger and greed, which can kill the Self to such an extent that there is no possibility of liberation from material entanglement.

Making Heaven on Earth

"Who told you, you are not already in heaven?" asks Sadhguru Jaggi Vasudev, "Why do you think there is another place which is better than this?" and advises, "One must see how to make a heaven out of himself or herself ... because the basis of your experience is within you. If you take charge of that, you can make heaven out of it right now. Your intolerant neighbour, the noisy child next door, your mother-in-law, all these people have been added so that there is a little spice in your life – for excitement – but it is actually heaven." So, it is really up to us to make a heaven or hell of our own existence on earth.

The Idea of Reincarnation

Reincarnation is known as *punar janma* in Sanskrit, which literally means rebirth. This is becoming a popular subject of conversation in the West. Sometimes in jest, when people say "See you in the next life" or "I must have known you in the past life" they unknowingly refer to reincarnation.

Necessity of Reincarnation

Hindu scriptures have advocated since time immemorial that the soul is immortal and keeps reentering a body, time and time again, in order to evolve from immaturity to spiritual illumination and to reap the good and bad consequences of the deeds of the previous births. The theories of karma and reincarnation occupy a very significant place in Hindu philosophy. They provide the most satisfactory answers to the numerous complex questions on seemingly unjustified suffering and inequality among human beings.

God does not give us karma, we create our own karma. According to karma doctrine, bad karma occurs because we have done something bad in the past to someone and now someone is doing something bad to us. Likewise, good karma means we have done something good in the past and others are now doing something good to us. This corresponds to the popular phrase: "What goes around, comes around." Your karma or deeds may have been done in the immediate past or the remote past. You may or may not remember it. It survives in the form of a seed within you. It takes time for the karmic seed to sprout. How and when this happens is unknown, but it is a fact that no one can escape their karma. That's the belief.

In the spiritual world, every action may not produce a reaction as quickly as it happens in the physical world. Sometimes, even a lifespan may not be sufficient to bring about the appropriate result of an effort, but sometime or the other it is bound to occur according to the law of karma. In such cases, it becomes necessary for the individual to take another birth to bear the consequences of their deeds in the previous births. For example, if one did an act of kindness just before they died, when would they reap the benefit of the good karma? Obviously, it will be returned to them as an act of kindness in the next life. Thus, the theory of karma leads to the theory of reincarnation. It is believed that a person is born again and again to reap the fruits of their own actions.

How Does Reincarnation Work?

The moral consequences of all actions are stored in Nature. If a person lives a good life on Earth, they will be born into a better life in the next incarnation. A person who leads an immoral life, it is believed, will be reborn as a poor human being in an agonizing environment in the next incarnation. Thus, we are constantly creating our own karma and determining the character of our next birth. We may be handicapped by our past deeds, but we are definitely the master of our future.

Can You Be Reborn as an Animal?

Here, another myth regarding karma and reincarnation can be eliminated. It is believed that once the soul attains a human body in the process of its normal evolution from the lower to the higher form of life, it will always assume a human body in the subsequent incarnations, regardless of the qualities of the past karma. In other words, it is not possible for a human being to be reborn as an animal.

Once the soul attains a human body, it will keep on assuming human bodies in the following births. Why? How else will they enjoy the fruits of good karma or feel the pains of bad karma in the future incarnations? Animals cannot differentiate between good and bad feelings in the same manner as human beings. Moreover, if they are reborn as an animal, their karmic cycle will stop and they will never achieve their final goal—that is liberation or salvation from the cycle of birth and death, commonly referred to as *moksha* or *nirvana* in Hinduism.

According to the Hindu scriptures, liberation or *moksha* is the birthright of every individual. It is the individual who is responsible for one's own *moksha* or salvation. No savior or redeemer can achieve this task for them. The concept of *moksha* or liberation in Hindu religion is of great moral and ethical significance, for it provides an incentive for righteous living in the world.

Adi Shankaracharya and Advaita Vedanta

When Adi Shankaracharya took birth, India was wallowing in a dark pit of decadence. Buddhism and Jainism had lost their pristine glory. Corrupt practices had crept into Hinduism. People could not turn to the existing modes of Hinduism for solace, purpose or direction. In the name of the *Vedas,* various sects of Hinduism tried to propagate travesties rather than the truths of the Vedic religion.

Adi Shankaracharya had a panoramic view of this when he wrote in his *Gita Bhashya:* "Finding the texts being interpreted in all sorts of contradictory and conflicting ways." This was to silence the impostors who deliberately twisted the texts that he had written, especially the *Prasthana Traya Bhashya* and other illuminating treatises. Shankara's rational commentaries undid, at once, the bad influence of the misinformed Hindu interpreters. He gave coherence to the body of these texts and won acceptability for his doctrine known as *Advaita Vedanta.*

Adi Shankaracharya, in the words of Pandit Jawaharlal Nehru, was "a curious mixture of a philosopher and a scholar, an agnostic and a mystic, a poet and a saint, and, in addition to all this, a practical reformer and an able organizer." He debated with relentless logic and outwitted the deluded through scholarly interpretations of Vedic texts. He silenced the misinformed people with convincing arguments against Vedic authority. He, thus, revitalized Hinduism.

What is the Philosophy of Advaita Vedanta?

Advaita means non-dualism and *Vedanta* means the

conclusion of the *Vedas*. Adi Shankaracharya postulated four central doctrines in his philosophy.

1. *Brahman*, the Absolute, is the ultimate reality. In *Brahman*, the distinction between the knower, knowledge, the objects to be known, the subject, and the means by which they are cognized, dissolves.

2. The world is not unreal as long as we are in it and are a part of it. But it becomes irrelevant and illusory when a higher perception of the *Brahman* is attained.

3. *Brahman* can be realized by following a four-fold path:
    - *Viveka*: right discrimination between the permanent and the impermanent, the real and the unreal;
    - *Vairagya*: detachment from sensory attractions;
    - *Sama, Dama and Shraddha*: calmness, self-control and faith; and
    - *Mumukshutva*: the constant yearning to attain moksha liberation from the finiteness of individuality.

4. *Bhakti* or Devotion is only a step to secure the grace of God; this obliterates the distinction between the aspirant and God.

The above doctrines can be summed up in three short statements of Adi Shankaracharya:

Brahma Satyam

Jagan Mithya

Jivo Brahmaiva Na Parah.

This translates roughly as follows:

God alone is real,

The world is unreal,

The individual is none other than God.

This means that there is only one Supreme Reality or *Brahman*, the Supreme Being. *Brahman* is infinite and omnipresent. Therefore, nothing can be added to it. Furthermore, there cannot be a place where he is not present. There is no place for the world, man or any creature outside the *Brahman*. It transcends all pairs of opposites and descriptions.

The reality of the world is then relative as opposed to the absolute nature of Brahman. In that sense and in comparison with *Brahman*, the world is unreal, very much like a dream, which has its own subjective reality, and illusory compared with the waking state.

The last of the three statements above asserts that the true nature of every individual is the *Brahman*. Because of *avidya*, i.e., our original and inherent spiritual ignorance, we have forgotten our true identity and we mistakenly believe that we are little, limited individuals.

Brief Life with the Productivity of Several Lives

Adi Shankaracharya lived for just thirty-two years. But, during the brief span, he did the work of several long lives put together. Lord Krishna gave the standing promise in the Gita to reinstate the majesty of the moral law whenever it declines. Accordingly, great souls come to this world periodically to fulfill the needs of the times. Adi Shankaracharya's advent called for the ruthless banishment of the wrong ideas about Hinduism with the superiority of intellect, reason and logic.

When Adi Shankaracharya was born, India was going through great intellectual, spiritual and social turmoil. Hinduism or Vedic religion had become a mere performance of elaborate rituals. The Hindu religion had given way to many intolerant sects each with thousands of deities. There were squabbles, dissension, and corruption in the name of religion.

It was into this fuming confusion and decadence that Adi Shankaracharya started pouring the life-giving, purifying and unifying philosophy of *Advaita Vedanta*. Ever since then, the Hindu religion, in spite of all its superficial differences in worship and practice, has been anchored in the all-comprehensive and non-sectarian philosophy of *Advaita Vedanta*. It is a philosophy that is intellectually acceptable and spiritually satisfying.

Because of these great reforms, the followers of Hinduism have never suffered from the conflict of which deity to worship. All gods and goddesses are revered and worshiped by them because Adi Shankaracharya's philosophy is one of inclusion and not exclusion. Hinduism survived mainly due to his philosophy, which continues to represent the dazzling and effulgent efflorescence of Hinduism. During his brief life of thirty-two years, Adi Shankaracharya accomplished his life's mission of giving the succeeding generations the distilled essence of the Vedic and Upanashadic truths.

ॐ॰ ॐ ॰ॐ

II
Goodness of the Scriptures

What we can apply in our everyday life from the teachings of Hindu holy texts

Immensity of the Vedic Scriptures

Unlike other religions, there is no single book that can be called the Vedic or Hindu scripture, which everyone considers their holy book. There is no one Hindu Bible. However, for centuries the *Bhagavad Gita* or simply referred to as the Gita, has been considered the holy scripture of the Hindus. This is why in the courts of law, the *Bhagavad Gita* is used to take oath by the Hindus – just like the Koran is used by the Muslims and the Bible by the Christians. This is because it contains the essence of all the Hindu scriptures. However, honestly speaking, Hindu do not know which book they may term as their scripture. This dilemma is due to the immensity of the Vedic scriptures. In this unit, I will attempt to familiarize you with the main Vedic scriptures.

The Shruti and Smriti

Two types of sacred writings constitute the Vedic scriptures. The first one is called *Shruti*, which means 'that which has been heard'. The second one is called *Smriti*, meaning 'that which has been memorized'.

Ancient Hindu saints, who led a solitary life in the woods, developed a consciousness that enabled them to hear or cognize the truths of the universe. Shruti literature has two parts: the Vedas and the Upanishads.

The Vedas

There are four Vedas— *Rig Veda* (royal knowledge), *Sama Veda* (knowledge of chants), *Yajur Veda* (knowledge of sacrificial rituals) and *Atharva Veda* (knowledge of incarnations). The four Vedas are the primary texts of the spiritual and religious records of the ancient culture and teachings of India. These teachings are based upon the recognition of the sacred nature of all life forms and self-realization as the true goal of human life.

The Vedas Are Also Referred to as:

- *Apaurushey*: meaning not 'authored by a *purusha* (human being)'. This means the Vedas are of divine origin, i.e., spoken by God.
- *Anadi*: without beginning (in terms of time)
- *Nishwasitam*: meaning 'the breath of God'. The Vedas, spoken by God, are called *Nishwasitam*.

As a cultural way of life, the Vedas represent a tradition that accepts all valid approaches to truth and embody the principles of universality and diversity.

In Vedic culture, self-realization is not limited to the teachings of any one savior or one holy book. There is no attempt to limit the truth to one particular form, approach or belief. Every individual is encouraged to discover the truth for himself/herself, and no attempt is made to dictate what the truth is supposed to be.

The Vedas prescribe rituals and meditations for attaining harmony in life. The rituals are intended to keep one's daily actions in harmony with divine will; the mediations are prescribed to realize one's true identity. The ritualistic parts of the Vedas are called *karmakand* (rituals) and the meditation portion of the Vedas is called the *gyankand* (knowledge).

The Upanishads

The cream of the Vedas is the Upanishads. The Upanishads are the divine revelations received by ancient saints and seers. They represent the essence of the Vedas, the greatest truths ever known to mankind. The Upanishads are arguably humanity's most profound philosophical enquiry. They are the first perceptions of the unity of everyone, the oneness of the individual and reality.

The basic teaching of the Upanishads is that the perfect human being, who has reached the pinnacle of awareness through meditation, is the divine spirit called the Brahman. The true nature of an individual is this divine spirit. There is only one being and one reality. In the words of the Upanishads, *tat tvam asi* (that thou art).

Let us understand the word 'Upanishad.' It consists of three parts: *up* – meaning 'near', *ni*, which means 'down', and *shad* meaning 'sit'. Thus, the word 'Upanishad' means 'sitting near a teacher and receiving secret teachings'. Free from theology and dogma, the Upanishads remain the primary source of inspiration and guidance for millions of Hindus and non-Hindus alike. They have influenced many Western philosophers, including Johann Wolfgang, Von Goethe, Arthur Schopenhauer, Ralph Waldo and Emerson.

There are 108 Upanishads of which eleven are the most important. They are:

1. Iso Upanishad
2. Kena Upanishad
3. Katha Upanishad
4. Prasna Upanishad
5. Mundaka Upanishad
6. Mandukya Upanishad
7. Aitareya Upanishad
8. Taittiriya Upanishad
9. Svetasvatara Upanishad
10. Chhandogya Upanishad
11. Brhadaranyaka Upanishad

The above Upanishads are also the concluding portions of the Vedas, commonly known as Vedanta. They focus on philosophical matters such as the purpose of life, origin of the universe, concepts of time, space and matter, and the concepts of *aatman* (soul), *Brahman* (God), *maya* (illusion), immortality, rebirth, karma and the universe. According to Max Muller "The conception of the world as deduced from the Vedas and chiefly from the Upanishads is indeed astounding."

The *Bhagavad Gita*

The *Bhagavad Gita* is derived from the great epic Mahabharata, which is considered by many scholars as the fifth Veda. The *Bhagavad Gita* is the essence of the Upanishads, not because it is in a condensed form, but because it makes the Vedanta philosophy easy to understand. If the Upanishads are compared to cows, the *Bhagavad Gita* is akin to the cows' milk. When one has plenty of milk at one's disposal, one need not undergo the laborious task of maintaining cows. One who has studied and understood the *Bhagavad Gita* is said to have understood the cardinal teachings of the Upanishads.

In the *Bhagavad Gita*, the *shruti* and *smriti* are blended. Because it is an exhaustive collection of spiritual laws, the Gita is called a *shruti*. When the spiritual laws are applied in life, it is called the Sanatana Dharma of eternal order and righteousness. Sometimes, the *Bhagavad Gita* is therefore referred to as 'the Bible of Vedic Dharma'.

As stated before, *smriti* means that which is remembered. *Smriti* scriptures are derived from the Vedas and are considered to be of human origin and not of divine origin like the Vedas and the Upanishads. They were written to explain and elaborate the Vedas, making them understandable and more meaningful to the general population. All authoritative writings outside the Vedas and *Bhagavad Gita* are collectively referred to as *smriti*. There are six important *smriti* scriptures that every Hindu should know of:

Dharmashastras: They describe the codes of the human conduct, righteousness, personal hygiene, social administration, ethical and moral duties. The best known *dharmashastra* is the *Manu Smriti*, the codes of conduct developed by Sage Manu. Manu prescribed Hindu conduct on the basis of self-control, non-injury, compassion and non-attachment—the prerequisites of a just and virtuous society. Therefore, *Manu Smriti* is a code of law for righteous living, which continues to dominate Hindu ethics even today.

Puranas: A wealth of the mythological knowledge is found in the *Puranas*, which contain information on incarnations, cosmology, creation, genealogy of kings and time cycles. Veda Vyasa is credited with the compilation of the Vedas and the *Puranas*. The purpose of the *Puranas* is the same as that of the *Itihasas*. They explain the Vedic principles and the ethics and rituals of religion with examples and parables for the consumption of the common man. Another purpose of the *Puranas* is to instill in a feeling of devotion and worship in people. There are 18 main *Puranas* and an equal number of subsidiary *Puranas*.

The main *Puranas* are:

1. Vishnu Purana
2. Naradiya Purana
3. Shrimad Bhagavata Purana
4. Garuda (Suparna) Purana
5. Padma Purana
6. Varaha Purana

7. Brahma Purana

8. Brahmanda Purana

9. Brahma Vaivarta Purana

10. Markandeya Purana

11. Bhavishya Purana

12. Vamana Purana

13. Matsya Purana

14. Kurma Purana

15. Linga Purana

16. Shiva Purana

17. Skanda Purana and

18. Agni Purana

The most popular among the *Puranas* is the *Shrimad Bhagavata*. It is a chronicle of the various incarnations of Lord Vishnu and focuses on Lord Krishna. Each *Purana* has a specific purpose and was first narrated on a special occasion. The purpose of the *Shrimad Bhagavata* is to enable a person to overcome the fear of death. Sukhdev Muni, the son of Veda Vyasa, narrated it to King Parikshit, when Parikshit was cursed to die in a week's time. The longest *Purana* is the Skanda Purana, which has 81,000 couplets. The shortest is the Markandeya Purana, which has 9,000 couplets.

Epics or the Ithihasas: The two great epics of Hindu religion are the Ramayana and the Mahabharata. These are the most popular spiritual books among the Hindus.

The Ramayana was originally written by Sage Valmiki. The story describes how Lord Vishnu appeared on Earth as Lord Rama and killed the demon king Ravana, who had oppressed his kingdom through his lust for power. The epic illustrates the ideal conduct in personal, social and public life. The Ramayana also illustrates the ideals of brotherhood, friendship, and chastity for both men and women.

The Mahabharata was written by Veda Vyasa; it is sometimes also referred to as the fifth Veda because of its deep influence on Hindus from all walks of life. It's a story of a great war that took place between the Kauravas and the Pandavas for the ownership of the ancient kingdom of Kurukshetra. In the battlefield of Kurukshetra, Lord Krishna was the charioteer of Arjuna (one of the Pandavas), who, upon seeing his friends and relatives gathered on the other side of the battlefield, told Krishna that he was not prepared to kill his own kith and kin for the sake of a kingdom. This led to an immortal dialogue between Arjuna and Lord Krishna, known as the *Bhagavad Gita*. The message of the Gita is universal and includes the basic beliefs of the Vedic religion.

Agmas **(or** *Tantras*): The *tantras* are the sectarian scriptures of the three major theological traditions of Hindu religion, namely Vaishnavas, Shaivas and Shaktas. The Vaishnavas adore Lord Vishnu as the ultimate reality as Lord Vishnu, the Shaivas revere Lord Shiva and the Shaktas venerate the divine mother of the universe as their ultimate reality. Each *agma* consists of four parts. The first part includes philosophical and spiritual knowledge. The second part covers yoga and mental discipline. The third part specifies rules for the construction of temples and sculpting the statues and figures of deities for worship in the temples. This is where all the idol shapes came from. The fourth part includes the rules pertaining to the observance of religious rights, rituals and festivals.

Darshanas **(Philosophies)**: The religious literature in this category can be classified into two divisions—heterodox and orthodox. The heterodox reject the authority of the Vedas; they include the Buddhists, Jains and Charvakas. The orthodox school accepts the Vedas and the Vedic literature as authoritative. There are six orthodox schools: Two *Mimansa* schools (*Purava Mimansa* and *Uttara Mimansa*) directly based on Vedic literature; the *Nyaya*, *Vaisheshika*, *Sankhya* and *Yoga* schools are based on slightly different ideology but they are consistent with the Vedas. Each *darshana* or school has writings attributed to its founder; each *darshana* has a number of commentaries written later by the followers of these schools.

Yogvashistha: It is the dialogue between Lord Rama and his guru Sage Vashistha. It comprises 29,000 Sanskrit verses, said to have been written by Sage Valmiki, who wrote the epic Ramayana (refer above). In poetic language and through curious stories and philosophical discourses, *Yogvashistha* expounds the Vedanta philosophy with seemingly more emphasis on the *Audwatic* doctrine of the Vedanta philosophy. *Audwatic* means 'no distinction between the human being and the supreme *Brahman*'.

Veda Vyasa: Protector of the Vedas

The full moon day of *Ashadh,* the fourth month of the Hindu year (*Vikram Samvat*), is also called *Vyasa Purnima,* as it is the birth anniversary of Sage Vyasa. It is to him we owe the Vedas, which were codified and handed down to us. Had he not reproduced the Vedas about 5,000 years ago, we would have lost the teachings of the four Vedas, which were revealed by Lord Brahma to a few rishis centuries ago. The Hindus, therefore, refer to Vyasa as Veda Vyasa and consider him to be the supreme guru. They celebrate his birth anniversary as *Guru Purnima.*

Biography of Veda Vyasa

Veda Vyasa, the son of Rishi Parashar and Satyavati, is also known as Krishna Dwaipayna, because he was dark complexioned and was born on an island or *dwipa*. He took birth at the end of the *Dvapara* Yuga, the time of King Shantanu, the grandfather of the Pandavas. To him is also attributed the fact that he continued the line of his mother and that Dhritrashtra, Pandu and Vidura were his progeny.

At a very tender age, Vyasa told his parents the secret of his life—he would have to go to the forest for penance. At first, Vyasa's mother did not agree to this; but she later gave him permission on the condition that he would appear before her whenever she wished for his presence.

Vyasa undertook initiation under his twenty-first guru, Sage Vasudeva. He studied the *Shastras* under the sages Sanaka, Sanandana and others. Vyasa was also called Vadrayan because he lived for some time in the jungles of *badari* in the Himalayas near Badrikashram.

An Incarnation of Lord Vishnu

Veda Vyasa is also considered to be one of the 24 incarnations of Lord Vishnu. In a prayer to Vyasa, the Hindus often recite:

Vyasay vishnuroopaya vyasroopay vishnave, Namo vai brhamanidhaye vaasishthaay namo namah.

The above prayer can roughly be translated as:

Hail thee, Vyasa, again and again,

Thou Vishnu in human frame,

Thou scion of Vasistha's ancient race,

It is from Thee that all knowledge springs.

According to Swami Shivananda, "Vyasa is considered by all Hindus as a *chiranjivi*, one who is still living and roaming around the world for the wellbeing of his devotees. It is said that he appears to the true and faithful, that Adi Shankara had his *darshan* in the house of Sage Mandana Misra, and that he appeared in front of many others as well. Thus, in short, Vyasa lives for the welfare of the world. Let us pray for his blessings on us and the whole world."

Lord Krishna, while disclosing His godhood to Arjuna, singled out Vyasa from all his contemporaries by declaring "among the sages, Vyasa is me."

Literary Creations of Vyasa

In addition to compiling the four Vedas, Vyasa wrote the *Brahma Sutras*. These *sutras* (clues for memory) tell you the real nature of the *Brahman*. The oldest commentary on the *Brahma Sutras* is by Adi Shankaracharya.

Vyasa also wrote the fifth Veda, the *Mahabharata*, the largest Hindu epic. The *Bhagavad Gita* is a small part of the *Mahabharata*.

According to a legend, *Mahabharata* was such a huge book that it needed a divine mind to write it correctly while Vyasa dictated it. Lord Ganesha was that divine mind. Vyasa also wrote seventeen *Puranas* or traditional stories of gods and goddesses, and 18 *Upapuranas*. He also reproduced the Ramayana, which was originally written by Sage Valmiki during the incarnation period of Lord Rama.

Vyasa's last work was the *Bhagavatam*, which he undertook at the instigation of Devarishi Narada who once came to him and advised him to write the *Bhagavatam* as, without it, Vyasa's goal in life would not be reached. His goal was the selfless surrender to the Supreme God with faith and devotion.

The Gita's Relevance in Modern Times

There is no doubt that modern men and women are far ahead of the older generation in terms of material possessions, affluence, and the knowledge of science, space and technology, but all this has been achieved at a terrible price. Men and women today have become restless and uneasy souls in the quest for contentment, peace and harmony. The questions that arise are: Is there any practical solution to achieve supreme glory and happiness? Are there easy practices in the midst of hurried goals, disputes and distractions of contemporary life? Precisely in response to these queries, I have decided to talk about the relevance of the Gita in modern times.

The *Bhagavad Gita* guides the lives of people all over the world in modern times. Mahatma Gandhi regarded it as a mother to whom the children (humanity) turned to when in distress. In the world of literature, there is no book so elevating and inspiring as the Gita. It is a universal scripture for people of all temperaments and for all times.

The Essence of the Gita

There are people with three kinds of temperaments—active, emotional and rational. So, there are three *yogas*—*Jnana Yoga* for the man of enquiry and self-analysis with a rational temperament, *Bhakti Yoga* for the man of emotional temperament and *Karma Yoga* for the man of active temperament. One *yoga* is as efficacious as the other. The Gita formulates the theory of the three paths—that of *jnana* (knowledge), *bhakti* (devotion) and *karma* (action). According to the teachings of the Gita, there is no conflict among the three. The Gita harmonizes the philosophy of action, devotion and knowledge. All three must be blended harmoniously if one wishes to attain perfection.

Gita as the Anodyne for the Restless Soul

The Gita's wisdom and practical teachings have many an answer to our condition of restlessness that is common in today's society.

The *Bhagavad Gita* is a message addressed to each and every human being to help them solve the vexing problem of overcoming the present and progressing towards a bright future. This Holy Scripture is not just a book of spiritual teachings, it transcends the bounds of religion and race. It is divine wisdom for humanity, in order to help us face and solve the problems of birth and death, pain, suffering, fear, bondage, love and hate. It enables us to liberate ourselves from all limiting factors and reach the state of perfect inner balance, inner stability, mental peace, and complete freedom from grief, fear and anxiety. Within Gita's 18 chapters lies the truth of human existence. The Gita talks about the experiences of everyone in this world, the drama of the ascent of human beings from a state of utter dejection, sorrow, breakdown and hopelessness to a state of perfect clarity, understanding, renewed strength, and triumph.

Each chapter contains an invaluable lesson and imparts a new understanding in a marvelous way. The mystery of the man, the world and God is explained in a lucid manner that one cannot find anywhere else. The workings of the human mind, the real problems to their welfare and happiness, the ways to overcome them, the path to blessedness, the path to eternal death, the secret of self-mastery, and the way to find peace amidst human duties and activities are contained in this great treasure. All this and more...

The Gita is not merely an excellent repository of ancient wisdom and esoteric oriental mysticism. Take for example the concept of yoga, which is India's pride, as described in the Gita. Yoga, according to the Gita, is not a mystic word or an impracticable term, but is a simple lesson on the duty of life, which is easy for men and women to practice without resorting to reclusion, austerity and renunciation of duties and obligations to families, communities and countries. Yoga can be adopted and absorbed as a habit in one's daily routine and existence. It can be practiced even in spite of and amidst the challenges and pressures of everyday life.

No other book does so much of plain-talking on topics such as yoga, karma, and attainment of happiness.

The Gita's Analysis of Anger

In the *Bhagavad Gita*, Chapter 2 verses 62 and 63, Lord Krishna analyzes anger in clear terms:

"When a man thinks of the objects, attachment to the object arises: from attachments desire is born; from desire anger rises; from anger comes delusion; from delusion the loss of memory; from loss of memory the destruction of discrimination; from destruction of discrimination a man perishes."

Loss of Reasoning

When we lose our temper, we lose our reasoning too, and when we lose our reasoning, we become animals. We have all learnt from our sad experience that when our temper flies, we never do anything we are proud of. We often end up apologizing for the same. However, an apology does not help curb our anger. In fact, by saying that you are sorry, you have just justified your deeds done in anger. In other words, you have found an excuse to be angry again.

Anatomy of Anger

The Gita tells us to first recognize how anger works. Anger is always associated with the frustration of not being able to fulfill your desires like greed, sexual pleasure, money, power and prestige. When you cannot get what you want, your mind gets disturbed and this results in anger, which takes your mind away from the real issue. Consequently, your sanity is affected. The trigger for anger could be trivial, but in no time your anger reaches its peak, thus destroying your power to discriminate. You do not care who you are hurting or harming. If you are unable to harm those you wish to harm, then you start harming or hurting yourself. That is what the Lord meant by saying that the end result of anger is one's own annihilation.

Anger is unbiased towards age, race, color, creed and religion. No person is exempt from it. It rouses even those who are by nature gentle and leads people to commit acts of savagery and violence.

Control of Anger

Now that you have understood how powerful and ruinous anger is, I am giving you three tips to avoid anger and its ugly consequences:

1. Remember that anger is not always bad as long as you have not lost your discriminating power. How do you recognize this? You do so by not being stubborn about fulfilling your desires.

2. Every evening, set aside ten minutes before going to sleep. Lay before the mind all the consequences connected with your anger and judge their real values. Remember that you cannot afford to become angry without losing something. Anger brings grief to a father, divorce to a husband or wife, failure to an employee and a loss to a businessman, and so on.

3. Read the 62nd and 63rd verses of Chapter 2 of the Gita every day in the morning and pray to the Lord to help you understand the true meaning of what He wishes to convey to us through these verses. Your prayer will definitely be answered one day. When that happens, you may still get angry occasionally but you will not be stubborn.

The Gita's Karmayoga: A Difficult Discipline

According to the Gita, *karmayoga* is present in the renunciation of both the fruit of karma and the attachment for karma. However, in the present age, there are not many *karmayogis* who can satisfy the test of the Gita. There are not many 'saints' and social workers, who can explain and illustrate by their own example how karma may be performed without any reference or attachment to its fruit and whose conduct may be accepted as ideal for guiding us along the path of *karmayoga*.

Theory vs. Practice

Karmayoga as enunciated in the Gita, appears to be a very difficult discipline to practice. Is this *karmayoga* a mere theoretical proposition or can it be actually practiced? If it can be practiced, there must be people who practice it. How can it be called an easy to practice discipline if there is no one that I know of who knows and practices the discipline?

The Gita Describes Three Types of *Karmayoga*:

1. *Karmayoga* that is present in the renunciation of attachment and the fruits of karma (Gita II.48);

2. *Karmayoga* in the renunciation of attachment towards all karma and objects (Gita VI.4) and

3. *Karmayoga* in the renunciation of the fruit of all karma (Gita XVIII.11) / the absence of craving for the fruit of karma (Gita VI.1).

In as far as the doctrine of *karmayoga* is concerned, there is no fundamental difference in the above three definitions. *Karmayoga* exists in the renunciation of both the fruit of karma and the attachment to the karma itself. Hence, it was appropriate for the Gita to mention both these forms of renunciation while defining *karmayoga*. In the renunciation of the attachment to karma and object, the other form of renunciation is also implied, though not expressly stated. For example, when the desire for wealth, honor and fame is renounced, the quest for them, i.e., the fruit of action, is automatically relinquished.

Difficulty in Practicing *Karmayoga*

Lord Krishna stated in the Gita (IV.2) that for a long time the practice of *karmayoga* had disappeared from this world. This shows that even in His own time, there were not many people who understood this yoga. In the present age too, there are not many who understand it. People fail to understand the secret of *karmayoga* as described by the Gita as their heart is torn by conflicting emotions such love and hatred. The secret of *karmayoga* is known only to those blessed souls whose sins have been washed away by the performance of selfless deeds.

It cannot be said that the real *karmayogis* are no longer present in this world. The truth is, in the absence of faith and reverence, we fail to meet and recognize these people. Under such circumstances, when we do not find any person who can give us a practical demonstration of *karmayoga* through his or her conduct, the only course left to us is to keep before us the teachings of the Gita as our ideal and try to regulate our conduct according to the same.

The *karmayoga* described in the Gita is not a mere theoretical proposition, but it can actually be put into practice. It appears difficult to us only because of our ignorance of the secret of its performance, our attachment to the body and the objects of the world and lack of faith. But as a matter of fact it is not so difficult.

Through disinterested performance of the duties laid down by the scriptures, implicit faith in the words of the Gita, and conduct according to the Gita's directives, our attachment for the world will gradually disappear and the secret of *karmayoga* will gradually unfold itself to us. When attachment is completely destroyed and the secret of *karmayoga* is revealed to us, the practice of *karmayoga* will no longer appear difficult.

The Real Problem

The scriptures and saints exhort us with one voice to give up the desire for honor and fame, as they are exceedingly harmful. Nevertheless, when honor and praise are bestowed upon us, they bring joy to our heart and we develop attachment to them, which in its turn stimulates the desire to win the same again and again. Due to ignorance or lack of wisdom, we tend to serve our minor interests and neglect our greater and truer interests, i.e. supreme bliss and supreme peace. However, the real problem is that we have read a lot about supreme bliss and peace in books but we have never tasted it. Hence, we are not prepared to renounce worldly and transient pleasures and work for eternal joy, peace and freedom.

The Solution

We all know well and we have also experienced the fact that the fruits of all earthly wants are temporary. Yet we feel miserable when we are forced to relinquish them. Our devotion to our earthly interests has grown to such an extent that it does not allow us to perceive our true goal of eternal joy.

So, what is the solution?

We have to always remain conscious of our real interests and save ourselves from the lure of the destructive earthly wants. However, it is easier said than done. For example, before we start any work, the first thought that arises in our minds is what do we gain from this? Our thoughts are naturally directed towards our selfish interests. Therefore, this thought of self-interest should be banished the moment it arises in the mind, before we start any work. What we regard as a gain in the worldly sense is not a gain in the truest sense of the term. True gain is that which has a real existence and once gained, it is never lost. Such true gain is secured through renunciation of worldly gains. Therefore, thoughts of earthly and personal gain, which arise when we start any task, should be immediately discarded as it is the root of all evils. Nip it in the bud. Let it not take roots in your mind and heart. It is much easier to pluck out a weed than uproot a tree.

The discipline of *karmayoga* is easy for those who have surrendered themselves to God knowing that He is the real doer and we are merely His instruments.

The Gita's Techniques of Mind Control

The mind is the seat of feelings that are technically superior to the senses. But unfortunately, it is usually the senses that mould one's feelings. But for any spiritual exercise to succeed, the senses must be subdued first. For that to happen, their immediate bosses, the feelings, must be sufficiently good and strong. This means, the mind, which is the seat of those feelings, should be properly trained and strengthened. Though the mind is, by nature, very restless and uncontrollable, its disciplining assumes primary importance in the practice of earnest spirituality.

Kathopanishad says, "Know the soul as the rider and the body as the chariot to which the senses are yoked like horses. The mind works like the reins with which the charioteer, viz. the understanding holds the horses, i.e. the senses, in check. The road is the material world in which the senses move. If the reins are not held wisely and firmly, the senses, like wild horses, will get out of control, and the chariot will not reach the destination. But if the man is wise and controls his mind, the senses behave like good horses and the rider safely reaches the end of his journey."

The Gita's Techniques

In the *Bhagavad Gita*, Chapter 6, *shloka* 35, Lord Krishna says to Arjuna:

Asamsayam mahabaho mano durnigraham calamAbhyasena to kaunteya vairagyena ca grhyate.

"Doubtless O mighty armed, the mind is restless and hard to control but by practice and non-attachment, O son of Kunti, it can be controlled."

Lord Krishna, via Arjuna, has given us the secret of controlling our mind, which remains ever so restless. But before one strives to understand what Krishna is saying, one must be able to recall what Arjuna asked in the previous *shlokas*. In shlokas 33 and 34 of Chapter 6 of the *Bhagavad Gita*, Arjuna talks about the restless nature of mind. He tells the Lord that the mind is as hard to control as the wind. In the above cited *shloka*, the Lord tells Arjuna the technique to control the mind. The Lord agrees with Arjuna that the mind is not easy to control and then He gives Arjuna two important means to control the mind. The first one is 'practice' and the second one is 'non-attachment'.

Behind the Techniques

Now, let us try to understand these two techniques. Why do we find it hard to control the mind? We become a slave to the mind when we completely surrendered ourselves to the bent of our mind. But we can change our old habits if we have the will. The uncontrollable and restless mind can be controlled and made calm by earnest and persistent practice, i.e., a consistent attempt at achieving a goal.

Weaning the mind from its old habit of restlessness requires regular and persistent attempts to draw it towards someone who is always at peace, i.e., God. The mind becomes pacified when it is drawn towards God. However, Lord Krishna cautions that practice alone may not work because the mind runs after those objects to which it is attached. What should we do then?

Krishna gives us the second watchword: Non-attachment. How is this done? Tell your mind that you, as the soul, are its boss, and you have experienced the evils of attachments. You must remind the mind of these evils every time it wanders. Ask your mind what it achieved by running after worldly attachments. Was it pain or pleasure? Is there any worldly relationship that is not based on selfishness? Is there anything in the world that has given your mind everlasting pleasure? Remind your mind of all the sufferings due to attachments. Soon you will realize that when all the worldly attachments are put down through discrimination, the mind slowly, but surely, comes under control.

The essence of the Gita's message is that if we want to succeed in the practice of meditation to control our mind, we must learn the practice of non-attachment.

ॐ

The Three Debts of Life

The Vedic scriptures say that an individual is born with three debts. The debt to God is called *deva rin*. The debt to sages and saints is called *rishi rin*. The third debt is to one's parents and ancestors and it is called *pitri rin*. These three debts are like three mortgages in one's life; they are not like liabilities. This concept is an attempt by Hindu scriptures to create an awareness of one's duties and responsibilities.

Deva Rin

Deva rin implies that we must be thankful to God for sustaining our life from cradle to grave. We owe our every breath to God. He has provided us with the air we breathe, the milk in our mothers' breasts, the food that we eat, the environment that nourishes us, the parents who look after us, the mind, intellect and soul, which guide us. The list goes on and on. Every day, we receive God's blessings in one form or another. So, how can we repay God? We can do so by dedicating our life in the service of God.

To a Hindu, service of God means service to all mankind, regardless of caste, color and creed. Reverence for all forms of life, including plants and animals, and protection of the environment are important parts of this step. Service of God also includes the practice of non-violence, truthfulness, obeying scriptural injunctions, practice of self-control, purity of thought, and a respectful attitude towards others, especially elders. In Hindu culture, respect and reverence for the elderly is recognized as a partial repayment of the debt to God. The Taittiriya Upanishad declares that parents and teachers must be treated as gods. *Matri devo bhava, Pitri devo bhava, Acharya devo bhava.*

Rishi Rin

The second debt is the debt to sages and saints. Sages have given us a vast store of knowledge in the form of scriptures. The scriptural knowledge, which is a treasure of immeasurable value, is the heritage of every human being, not only the Hindus. However, much of the Vedic wisdom has not been yet explored and very little has been introduced to the people. Humanity at large is not aware of the great treasure that lies in the Hindu scriptures. The great wealth of knowledge related to psychology and parapsychology is in the *Rajayoga sutras*, commonly known as the yoga of meditation. There are profound insights and practical techniques to improve one's personality in the scriptures dealing with *Gyanayoga* (the yoga of wisdom), *Bhaktiyoga* (the yoga of devotion) and *Karmayoga* (yoga of action) and their numerous ramifications. How is this debt repaid? This debt can be paid by preserving and enriching the cultural heritage that is handed down from one generation to another. One should also donate generously towards community service and support the causes of the society by actively taking part in volunteering activities.

Pitri Rin

The third debt an individual is expected to pay during one's lifetime is to one's parents and ancestors. One's entire existence, the family name and the great dharma that one belongs to are the gifts of parents and forefathers. Just like your parents, who brought you into this world, protected you when you were weak and frail, fed you, clothed you, taught you, and even tolerated you, your grandparents performed similar duties for your parents.

Everything that one does in this world should enhance the fame and glory of one's family and forefathers. Everyone should conduct themselves in a manner that would make their parents and ancestors proud.

If someone in a family does great virtuous deeds, it is believed that the ancestors also rejoice in heaven. A son or a daughter, by their righteous actions, brings delight to the living parents and to the souls of the dead ancestors. It is the responsibility of everyone to keep up the pride of the family line by actions that promote the good of all. Only good actions and attainments can delight parents and forefathers. On the other hand, negative actions or sinful deeds displease the parents as well as the ancestors.

॥ ॐ ॥

What the Scriptures Say about Vegetarianism

In Hinduism, there are no commandments or rigid do's and don'ts about what we ingest. All Hindu scriptures tell us, "You are what you eat." They further state that the food we eat determines the temperament we possess. Accordingly, food is divided into three categories: *sattvic* (pure), *rajasic* (energizing), and *tamasic* (dull). The *sattvic* foods produce calmness and serenity of the mind; they include plants, vegetables, nuts, fruits, grains, pulses, and milk products. The *rajasic* foods contribute to the restlessness of the mind and include onions, garlic, peppers, spices and sour and bitter foods. The *tamasic* foods lead to the degeneration of human nature; they include meat, alcoholic beverages, and stale food.

Steven Rosen, in his famous book *Food for the Spirit, Vegetarianism and the World Religion* says: "Despite popular knowledge of meat eating's adverse effects, the non-vegetarian diet became increasingly widespread among the Hindus after two major invasions by foreign powers, first the Muslims and later, the British. With them came the desire to be 'civilized' and to eat, as did the *sahib*. Those actually trained in Vedic knowledge, however, never adopted a meat-oriented diet, and the pious Hindu still observes vegetarian principles as a matter of religious duty."

That vegetarianism has always been widespread in India is clear from the earliest Vedic texts. This was observed by the ancient traveler Megasthenes and also by Fa Hien, a Chinese Buddhist monk who, in the fifth century, traveled to India to obtain authentic copies of the scriptures. These scriptures unambiguously support the meatless way of life.

In the *Mahabharata*, the great warrior Bhishma explains to Yudhishtira, the eldest of the Pandava princes, that the meat of animals is like the flesh of one's own son and that the foolish person who eats the meat of animals must be considered the vilest of human beings [*Mahabharata*, Anu 114.11]. The eating of 'dirty' food, it warns, is not as terrible as the eating of flesh [*Mahabharata*, Shanti. 141.88]

The Manusmriti too declares that one should 'refrain from eating all kinds of meat,' for such eating involves killing and leads to karmic bondage [Manusmriti, 5.49].

Elsewhere in the Hindu scriptures, the last of the great Vedic kings, Maharajah Parikshit, is quoted as saying "only the animal killer cannot relish the message of the Absolute truth" [Shrimad Bhagvatam, 10.1.4].

Plants and Vegetables Have Life Too

Even the plants we eat have life and if non-violence is one of the arguments against eating meat, then we should not even eat plants and vegetables. We must realize that there is a difference between essential violence and non-essential violence. In order to survive in this world, we are required to destroy some life. As long as living involves the destruction of life, the killing of roots, vegetables and fruits involves the least pain and agony and therefore this type of food is recommended for the healthy growth of the body, mind and intellect.

Hinduism expects a human being to exercise compassion in deciding what they should or should not eat. Certain sects of Hinduism are known to perform excessive animal sacrifices because their level of compassion has diminished to the lowest point. Similarly, a few Vedic people were also meat eaters. Thus, depending upon the level of compassion, one may select certain foods and reject others.

Milk and Veganism

A cow is bestowed the status of a mother for its milk. Hence, cow's milk is considered to be *sattvic*, infused with mother's love. However, today's industrialized dairy farming has relegated cows to no more than economic assets that are exploited for maximum yield. The means of artificial insemination, separation of cows from calves right after birth, injection of bovine growth hormones for maximizing milk yield, and a constant state of lactation through incessant impregnation, are far removed from the principles of *ahimsa* or non-violence. Such milk, imbued with the pain and the atrocities, is likely to be more harmful than beneficial.

While Hinduism doesn't talk about veganism from the perspective of total abstinence from cow's milk, the principle of *ahimsa* advocates milk only from cows that are nurtured naturally, where the milk is in addition to the share meant rightfully for the calves -- only then one may consider such milk as a mother's blessing or gift of health.

Reasons to Adopt Vegetarianism

Although there is no direct scriptural reference in Hinduism against meat eating, save the injunction against eating beef, more than a third of all Hindus are vegetarians because of the following reasons:

1. The law of non-injury (*ahimsa*): It is the Hindu's first duty in fulfillment of his religious obligations to God and God's creation as defined by the Vedic scripture.

2. The law of karma: As Hinduism believes that all our actions, including our choice of food, have karmic consequences, we must in future experience the same amount of suffering inflicted on the creatures, even indirectly, by eating their meat.

3. The law of spiritual progress: What we ingest affects our consciousness, emotions and experiential patterns. By ingesting animal meat, one introduces into the body and mind negative emotions like anger, jealousy, fear, anxiety, suspicion and terrible fear of death, all of which are locked into the flesh of butchered creatures.

4. The law of good health: It has been proven by medical studies that vegetarians are less susceptible to all the major diseases that affect contemporary humanity and they thus live longer, healthier and more productive lives. They have fewer physical complaints, fewer visits to the doctor and fewer dental problems. Their immune system is stronger, their bodies are purer and more refined, and their skin is more beautiful.

5. The Law of Ecological Balance: Many of the world's massive ecological problems such as global warming, erosion of

topsoil, loss of rain forests and extinction of species have been traced to the single fact of meat in the human diet. Raising livestock for their meat is a very inefficient way to generate food. Pound for pound, far more resources must be expanded to produce meat than to produce grains, fruits, and vegetables.

III
Gods as Symbols

*What we can learn from the symbolism and
iconography of Hindu deities*

Goddess Lakshmi and Her Nine Symbols

Goddess Lakshmi is worshiped in India and around the world on Diwali, festival of lights for both worldly and spiritual prosperity. The word 'lakshmi' originates from the word *'laksya'* or *'laksma'*, which means 'goal'. Lakshmi, by semantic implications, is the goddess of the supreme goal. Another Sanskrit word *'laksha'* means a lac (lakh) or a hundred thousand.

Lakshmi is said to be Lord Vishnu's consort. The word 'Vishnu' is related to the word *'vishva'* (the created world) and it means 'one who is present in every atom of the creation'. Thus, Vishnu's consort has to have powers and majesty conducive to life and its maintenance. Lakshmi is the active principle, which helps Vishnu sustain creation.

Another name for Lakshmi is *'shri'*, which means grace and competence. It means the power of wealth, knowledge, purity and physical powers. The highest state of *shri* is always present in the *Brahman* (cosmic principle). He is known as Shripati, the Lord of Shri.

1. The Four Hands: Like in other deities, the four arms represent the four directions. It is a symbol of Lakshmi being omnipotent and omnipresent. The two frontal arms through the two frontal hands symbolize the activity in the objective world. The two back arms through the two hands at the back symbolize the activity at the subjective level. In Goddess Lakshmi's case, the upper-left back-hand represents *dharma* (duty). The lower-left frontal hand represents *artha* (material wealth). The lower-right frontal hand represents *kama* (desire) and the upper-back right hand represents *moksha* (salvation).

2. Half-open Lotus in Upper-left Hand: In the upper left hand, Goddess Lakshmi holds a half-blossomed lotus, which has a hundred petals. In philosophical terms, the number 100 represents the state of *sadhana*. This lotus represents *dharma* too. *Dharma* means one's duty or the task to which one is born in a particular time or place. In other words, it means 'one's allotted task'. Notice that this lotus is basically red. It is not in full blossom. It has streaks of white. The red in the lotus represents *rajoguna* (the functional aspect) and the white represents *satoguna* (the purity aspect). Activity and purity are two basic traits of *dharma*. In other words, the lotus symbolizes progress in both the mundane and spiritual walks of life side by side.

3. Gold Coins in Lower-left Hand: This hand of the goddess is shown dropping gold coins on the ground, where we find an owl sitting. The dropping of coins represents prosperity in all directions or total prosperity. The gold coins do not represent only money, they also symbolize prosperity at all levels.

4. *Abhaya Mudra* in Lower-right Hand: The right lower hand is held in *abhaya mudra* (the pose signifying assurance of freedom from fear). In Hindu philosophy, *kama* means both worldly and non-worldly desires. Unfulfilled desires cause fear, says the Gita. The ultimate gift of the goddess is the blessing of deliverance from fears.

5. Lotus in Upper-right Hand: This hand holds a fully open lotus with one thousand petals (in contrast to the upper left hand holding a half-open lotus with a hundred petals). This is synonymous with the *sahasra-ra-chakra* (the highest point in the evolution of the *Kundalini Shakti*). This lotus has a red base, with a blue tinge. The red represents *rajas* and the blue represents *akasha* (space). They signify total evolution.

Here it is significant to note that there are two frontal arms and two arms rising from the back of the two frontal arms. The frontal arms represent *preya marga*, the manifest, pleasant ways of the world. *Preya marga* represents *artha* (prosperity) and *kama* (desire). The other two back arms signify the *shreya marga* representing *dharma* (duty) and *moksha* (salvation). This cycle is subtle and conveyed to the seeker through four hands and arms, i.e. *dharma*, *artha*, *kama* and *moksha*, the four fold ambits of human endeavor (*purushartha*).

6. The Red Sari: Lakshmi is shown wearing a red sari. It is again the color of *rajas*, which means creative activity. The golden embroidery indicates plenty. This reaffirms the idea of prosperity in general. This is in keeping with Lakshmi being the goddess of prosperity.

7. The Lotus: The goddess is shown sitting on a lotus. This posture means 'live in the world, but do not be possessed by the world'. The lotus keeps smiling on the surface of the water. Its origin is in the mud, deep under water, but its flowering is above the surface of the water. Detachment and evolution is the message of this poetic symbol.

8. The Owl: The owl sitting on the left of Lakshmi, where gold coins are falling, represents darkness. The owl is a nocturnal bird and can't see clearly in the daytime. It represents perversion of attitudes in material prosperity. Undue attachment to wealth shows ignorance (darkness) and disturbs the economic balance in society. If man does not keep his balance when he gets a lot of material resources, he is bound to become a nuisance to himself and others around him.

9. Four White Elephants Pouring Water from Golden Vessels: In most pictures of Lakshmi, we see four white elephants pouring water drawn from the ocean on the goddess. This water is contained in golden vessels. The four elephants represent the four directions—North, South, East, and West. The white hue here means purity. Wisdom is occasionally represented in Hindu mythology in the form of an elephant.

The symbol of four elephants pouring water from golden vessels on the goddess suggests that the chain of *purushartha* (endeavor) must be continuously strengthened with wisdom, purity, and charity.

Goddess Lakshmi, thus, represents wealth and prosperity, and activities to attain liberation and self-realization.

Decoding Mother Durga's Symbols

The word 'Durga' in Sanskrit means 'a fort or a place which is difficult to overrun'. Another meaning of Durga comes from *durgatinashini* or the one who eliminates sufferings. Thus, the Hindus believe that the Goddess Durga protects her devotees from the evils of the world and removes their miseries.

Since time immemorial, Durga has been worshiped as the absolute power of the Supreme Being. She has been referred to as Parashakti in the early scriptures such as the *Yajurveda*, *Vajasaneyi Samhita* and *Taittareya Brahman*.

There are many incarnations of Durga. Her manifestations are countless. Kali, Bhagavati, Bhavani, Ambika, Lalita, Gauri, Kandalini, Java and Rajeswari are all her forms. She is the mother of the universe. The pious and the wicked, the rich and the poor, the saint and the sinner are all her children. She is Nature itself. She is the power behind the work of creation, preservation and destruction of the world. In short, she runs the show in this world.

Although Mother Durga represents cosmic energy and which is formless, the ancient authors of Indian mythology encoded this symbolic representation in the form of Mother Durga for us to realize her spiritual significance. The various physical attributes of Mother Durga undoubtedly represent a scientific effort of ancient artists and thinkers to convey philosophical wisdom with symbols so that the ordinary mind can understand her qualities. However, before we attempt to comprehend Durga's form and her symbols, we must recall an illuminating legendary work—*Devi Bhagavatam*. It says that Durga incarnated as the united power of all divine beings to kill the demon Mahishasura. These divine beings offered her various physical attributes and weapons. Let us now examine Devi Durga's composition and understand its symbolism.

1. Durga's Dress: Ma Durga wears a red dress. Red symbolizes activity. This is in keeping with the function she had to perform—kill Mahishasura. *Mahish* means 'male buffalo'; in order to destroy this buffalo-demon, Mahishasura had to be drawn out into the battlefield. The buffalo represents ego and the red dress symbolizes activity with knowledge, which is essential to destroy the demon of ego.

2. Ten Arms: They represent the 10 directions—namely East, Southeast, South, Southwest, West, Northwest, North, Northeast, upwards or top and downwards or bottom. This suggests that Durga protects the devotees from all directions.

3. The Three Eyes: Like Shiva, Mother Durga is also referred to as Triyambake, meaning 'the three-eyed goddess'. The left eye represents desire (moon), the right eye represents action (sun), and the central eye is knowledge (fire).

4. The Lion: It represents power, will and determination. The lion symbolizes the qualities required to meet the challenges of ego, which is very wicked. Lion is known for his regal habits and does not attack unless hungry. Mother Durga riding the lion symbolizes her mastery over all these qualities. This suggests to the devotee that he has to have all the above qualities in him if he wants to conquer the demon of ego.

5. The Conch Shell: The conch symbolizes the *pranava* or the mystic word 'om'. The sound that emanates from it is *omkar*. Mother Durga holding the conch in one of her eight hands indicates her holding on to God in the form of sound.

6. The Bow and Arrows: Arrows represent potential energy. An arrow can be released only with the help of a bow, which has to be pulled hard up to the ear. This is the process of converting potential energy into kinetic energy. By holding both the bow and arrows in one hand, Mother Durga indicates her control over both aspects of energy.

7. The Thunderbolt: This signifies firmness. The devotee of Durga must be firm like a thunderbolt in one's convictions. There is no scope for doubt. The thunderbolt can break anything that strikes against it, but it is not affected while striking. It is not affected by any challenge; so should the devotee be—unaffected by any difficulty.

8. The Lotus: The flower held by Mother Durga is not in full bloom. It symbolizes certainty of success but not finality. The lotus in Sanskrit is called *pankaj*, which means 'born of mud'. Thus, the lotus stands for continuous evolution of the spiritual quality of devotees amidst the worldly mud of lust and greed.

9. The Sudarshan Chakra: It literally means 'a beautiful discus.' This wheel moves around the index finger of the goddess. It does not touch her finger. No effort of Durga is involved in this movement. This signifies that the entire world-wheel is subservient to the will of Durga and is at her command. She uses this weapon unfailingly to destroy evil and create a beautiful environment for the growth of righteousness.

10. The Sword: Durga holds a shining sword in one of her eight hands. It is sharp and pointed. It symbolizes knowledge that has the sharpness of the sword. Its light weight teaches us that true knowledge does not sit heavily on anyone. The shining part of the sword stands for knowledge that is free from any doubt

11. The Trident: This is a symbol of three qualities: *satwa* (inactivity), *rajas* (activity) and *tamas* (dullness). By holding this in her hand, Durga conveys that the three qualities that make the worldly creatures are in her hands and she is beyond the three qualities. The trident or the *trishul* removes three types of miseries of the devotees—physical, mental and spiritual.

12. The Abhaya Mudra (Fearless Hand Gesture): The eighth hand of Mother Durga is held in the *abhay mudra*, the pose signifying assurance of freedom from fear. Through this pose, the universal mother tells her devotees to surrender all actions and duties to her so that she releases them from all fears.

Mother Durga has been shown in many forms with four, eight, twelve, and sometimes even eighteen hands. The instruments in her hands also differ in different pictures. They all have their own significance. However, the underlying purpose is the same—that is to convey to her devotees a great sense of security.

Hanuman: Simian Symbol of the Ideal Character

Both in Valmiki's Ramayana and Tulasidasa's *Ramcharitmanas*, Hanuman is a glowing symbol of service, devotion and dedication to the cause of his master, Lord Rama. From the moment he decides that Rama is God incarnate, Hanuman lives for Rama and Rama alone. He has no other interests in the world except the service of Rama, whom he completely identifies with.

Gyaninama Agreganyama: Foremost Among the Wise

Tulasidasa has described Hanuman as the foremost among the seers with supreme realization. Hanuman's great intellect has been recognized by Rama in various instances in the Ramayana. Take for example, the first meeting of Rama and Hanuman in the Kishkindhakand of the Ramayana. His speech to Rama is very interesting. Rama was greatly influenced by this speech and said to Lakshmana, "Such speech is possible only by a person who is well-versed in the Vedas, is a perfect grammarian and has deeply learnt social and ethical sciences." Now remember, Rama himself was thoroughly conversant with the Vedas, Upanishads and other scriptures. Therefore, his opinion of Hanuman cannot be dismissed lightly.

The Powerhouse of Strength

Despite Hanuman's established greatness and achievements in the domains of physical valor, intellectual character, tender humanism and spiritual excellence, it is not possible for many to get rid of the simian form or the monkey figure associated with him.

Does his figure with a long tail that wags so often indicate a lower stage in the Darwinian evolutionary process—a sub-human condition? No, nothing can be farther from the truth. Consider the following explanations and form your own opinion as to whether Hanuman was *nara* (human being) or *vanara* (monkey):

In the Ramayana, the various warlike races have been described as *vanaras* (monkeys), *bhaloos* (bears) and *rakshasas* (demons). These races used to don masks not only on their heads, but also on their bodies to look more formidable to their enemies. Some of them were masters of personification and disguise, and once they assumed the chosen form, they were beyond recognition. When one reads the Ramayana, it becomes evident that the secret of such an art was known to Hanuman. However, some of the *rakshasas* too were well-versed in the art. For example, Maricha assumed the form of a golden deer to allure Janaki, the wife of Rama. Ravana too disguised himself as a mendicant, when he appeared in Panchavati and kidnapped Janaki.

Hanuman was a complete master of yogic powers, which he could confer upon others too. There are records that show that even in the present age, a yogi with Hanuman's *siddhis* (powers) can assume any form. Hanuman could change his form at will, according to the demands of the occasion. He appeared before Rama and Lakshmana at Rishyamuka and before Vibhishana in Lanka—in the form of an ascetic and a learned Brahmin, respectively. He took a diminutive form in front of Janaki. He looked formidable to his adversaries and dreadful when he ransacked Lanka with his tail on fire.

Hanuman was *purushottama*, the highest form of a human being. The title of 'Purushottama' was conferred upon Hanuman by Rama, the Supreme Being himself. Therefore, thinking of Hanuman as just a loyal giant monkey is almost an act of sacrilege.

Let us look into some of Hanuman's unique strengths and traits.

Hanuman as a Friend: The friendship of Hanuman and Sugriva was like that of the wind and the fire. Hanuman never left Sugriva even in the worst of times. He remained his friend in good as well as adverse times.

Hanuman as a Great Diplomat: Rama had full faith in Hanuman's diplomacy and knowledge. When Vibhishana, the minister of an enemy kingdom and the brother of Ravana, came to Rama, a question arose whether to accept him as a friend or not. It was very difficult to ascertain the purpose with which Vibhishana had come to Rama. But Hanuman displayed diplomacy advising Rama to accept Vibhishana. Rama took his advice, and Vibhishana proved to be extremely valuable in killing Ravana.

Hanuman engulfing Lanka in flames was a political move. By burning Lanka, Hanuman had won half the battle. He struck terror in the minds of the people of Lanka. They lost confidence in themselves. And in a war, when the confidence of the people is shaken, half the battle is won. The terror-stricken people were left wondering how many mighty warriors like Hanuman was there in Rama's army.

Hanuman, a Humble Servant: 'Hanuman' literally means 'he who has demolished his ego'. Both Valmiki and Tulsidasa have beautifully described Hanuman's deep sense of selfless service. To show his gratitude, Rama asked Hanuman what he could do for him. Hanuman did not ask for salvation or a place in heaven. Instead he said, "I wish my respect and love for you never decreases. I should never contemplate anything else except you."

Tulsidasa says in *Hanuman Chalisa*:

Rama rasayana tumharey pasa, sada raho raghupati kay dasa

(Oh Hanuman, you hold the essence of devotion to Rama, always remaining his servant).

Hanuman remained intoxicated with Rama's nectar. He drew upon the yogic *siddhis* only when he was executing some great work to serve the Lord. He did so in a resigned manner, without any display of ego. Otherwise, he remained oblivious of his superhuman powers and had to be reminded of them from time to time.

When Hanuman leapt across the ocean, he constantly remembered his Lord, so that he would not trip mentally and convert his dedicated performance into a personal triumph. Hanuman teaches us one can achieve greatness through humble service. The boldness of Hanuman is his humility. The success of Hanuman lies in his deep sense of service to Rama.

In the final analysis, let me quote Tulsidasa again. *Sankat katey mitey sab peera, jo sumirey Hanumat balbira*. This means one who concentrates on Hanuman's character and applies it to his daily life, finds his misfortunes coming to an end; he is completely transformed and his inner self starts dominating over his pettiness, which in fact is the main cause of one's misfortunes.

ॐ

The Significance of Ganesha's Symbols

Ganesha is one of the most beloved of all deities in the Hindu pantheon. He is seen everywhere—from the sanctum sanctorum of the holiest shrines to the roadside temples. He adorns the shelves of devotees with his benign countenance. He resides permanently in the hearts of his countless devotees.

Ganesha's popularity stems from the fact that he is seen as generous in handing out good luck to everyone. He is a bit like Santa Claus. People like Ganesha because he is a nice guy. He represents the jovial part of human nature. He is a celebration of happiness and good living.

Ganesha and *Aum*

Lord Ganesha is both *Saguna Brahman* or having a form and *Nirguna Brahman* or beyond form. As *Saguna Brahman*, He is most commonly depicted as a strange composite of an elephant and a man, mounted on a mouse, with four arms. As *Nirguna Brahman*, He represents the *pranava* (*Aum*), which is the symbol of the Supreme Self. If you view Lord Ganesha sideways, as shown above, you will see the symbol *Aum* in Sanskrit. That's why Ganesha is called 'Aumkara' and is worshiped first by all Hindus regardless of their belief in *Saguna* or *Nirguna Brahman*.

Taitiriya Upanishad (1.8.1.) states, "*Aum iti Brahman* (*Aum* is *Brahman*)." Nothing can be done without uttering the word *Aum*. This further explains the practice of invoking Lord Ganesha before beginning any rite or undertaking any project.

Ganesha's Popularity around the World

Hundreds of years ago, Hindu missionaries went to different countries. They carried with them the idols of Ganesha who was their supreme deity. They spread their ideas about Ganesha's form and power and the symbolic significance of his form. Merchants used to carry the idols of Ganesha to foreign countries so that their journey and trade were free from obstacles. Thus, the people of foreign lands came to know about Ganesha. Today, Ganesha is a popular god even in foreign countries.

The Zoomorphic Image and Symbolism of Ganesha

Lord Ganesha symbolizes auspiciousness. As mentioned earlier Ganesha's image is a strange composite of an elephant and a man. Every part of His image is symbolic.

The elephant head of Lord Ganesha is the overseeing, all-seeing eternal witness, the unmanifest supreme. Below the head is the belly, the symbol of the manifest, the mortal.

Ganesha is the lord of all, manifest and unmanifest with the proverbial memory of an elephant. Ganesha's twisted trunk represents the zigzag path to wisdom. It reminds us that there is no direct path on which we must turn right and left in the search for truth.

The elephant's ears are like winnows that separate the wheat from the chaff. This symbolizes that all experience must be subjected to scrutiny to determine what is essential and what is nonessential. This is a critical aspect of judgment. The discerning and the wise do what they must and let the rest be.

Ganesha's endearing potbelly is equated with space. it is vast enough to hold all wisdom and all life. Gentle and harmless, He uses His great strength only when provoked.

Ganesha's vehicle, the lowly mouse, stands for the dark, fertile forces of the Earth into which it burrows itself to avoid light. As a recurrent threat to the harvest, it must be tamed. But the rat also represents swiftness of movement. He burrows with his sharp teeth, chews through anything, and squeezes out of the smallest of holes. He proves to be an excellent transport for Ganesha, who needs to be everywhere and anywhere at short notice to remove obstacles.

ॐ

The Symbolism of Saraswati

"May Goddess Saraswati,
who is fair like the jasmine-colored moon,
and whose pure white garland is like frosty dew drops;
who is adorned in radiant white attire,
on whose beautiful arm rests the veena,
and whose throne is a white lotus;
who is surrounded and respected by the Gods, protect me.
May you fully remove my lethargy, sluggishness, and ignorance."
Saraswati Vandana (Translated from Sanskrit)

Saraswati, the goddess of knowledge and arts, represents the free flow of wisdom and consciousness. She is the mother of the Vedas, and chants directed to her, called the 'Saraswati Vandana' often begin and end Vedic lessons. She is the daughter of Lord Shiva and Goddess Durga. It is believed that goddess Saraswati endows human beings with the powers of speech, wisdom and learning.

The Four Hands of the Goddess

Saraswati has four hands representing four aspects of human personality in learning: mind, intellect, alertness and ego. In visual representations, she has sacred scriptures in one hand and a lotus--the symbol of true knowledge--in the opposite hand.

With her other two hands, Saraswati plays the music of love and life on a string instrument called the veena. She is dressed in white--the symbol of purity--and rides on a white swan, symbolizing Sattwa Guna (purity and discrimination). Saraswati is also a prominent figure in Buddhist iconography--the consort of Manjushri.

Learned and the erudite individuals attach great importance to the worship of goddess Saraswati as a representation of knowledge and wisdom. They believe that only Saraswati can grant them moksha-- the final liberation of the soul.

Saraswati Stands for Knowledge and Wisdom

As Diwali--the festival of light--is to Lakshmi, goddess of wealth and prosperity; and as Navaratri is to Durga, goddess of power and valor; so is Vasant Panchami to Saraswati, the goddess of knowledge and arts.

Saraswati's birthday, Vasant Panchamis, is a Hindu festival celebrated every year on the fifth day of the bright fortnight of the lunar month of Magha.

Hindus celebrate this festival with great fervor in temples, homes and educational institutes alike. Pre-school children are given their first lesson in reading and writing on this day. All Hindu educational institutions conduct special prayer for Saraswati on this day.

The most significant aspect of Vasant Panchami is that it is also the most auspicious day to begin laying one's foundations of education--of how to read and write. Pre-school children are given their first lesson in reading and writing on this day, and all Hindu educational institutions conduct special prayer for Saraswati on this day.

It is also a great day to inaugurate training institutes and new schools--a trend made famous by the renowned Indian educationist, Pandit Madan Mohan Malaviya (1861-1946), who founded the Banaras Hindu University on Vasant Panchami day in 1916.

During Vasant Panchami, the advent of spring is felt in the air as the season undergoes change. New leaves and blossoms appear in the trees with the promise of new life and hope. Vasant Panchami also announces the arrival of another big springtime event in the Hindu calendar--Holi, the festival of colors.

Saraswati's favorite color, white, has a special significance on this day. Statues of the goddess are dressed in white clothes and are worshiped by devotees adorned with white garments.

ॐ

IV
Inner Strength

*How simple lessons from Indian traditions
can change our lives*

Ten Commandments for Peace of Mind

How does one attain peace of mind, which is the most sought-after commodity of humanity, especially in today's world of cutthroat competition? It appears that most of us are in a state of perpetual restlessness, despite the good healthcare systems and economic security that we enjoy.

Here are 'ten commandments' and they need to be followed religiously, with complete diligence, if one is serious about achieving perfect peace of mind.

1. Do not interfere in others' business unless asked to do so: Most of us create our own problems by interfering too often in others' affairs. We do so because somehow, we have convinced ourselves that our way is the best way and our logic is the most perfect logic, and those who do not conform to our way of thinking must be criticized and steered towards the right direction, which is essentially our direction.

This kind of attitude denies the existence of individuality and consequently the existence of God, for God has created each one of us in a unique way. No two human beings can think or act in exactly the same way. All men or women act the way they do because they are prompted to do so by the Divine within them. God looks after everything. Why are you so bothered about others' affairs? Mind your own business and you will enjoy peace.

2. Forget and forgive: This is the most powerful way to peace of mind. We often nurture ill feelings inside our heart for the person who insults or harms us. We foster grievances, which in turn results in loss of sleep, stomach ulcers, high blood pressure and many other ailments that stealthily gnaws us from within.

We nurture our grievance and keep digging our wound forever, though the insult or injury was done to us long ago. Therefore, it is essential to cultivate the art of forgiving and forgetting. Believe in the justice of God and the doctrine of karma. Let Him judge the act of the one who insulted you. Life is too short to waste in trifles. Forget, forgive and march on.

3. Do not crave for recognition: This world is full of selfish people. They seldom praise anybody without selfish motives. They may praise you today because you are rich and have power, but the moment you become powerless, they will forget your achievements and start criticizing you.

Remember, every person on earth is a mortal with a bundle of defects. No one individual is perfect. Then why do you value the words of praise of another mortal like you? Why do you crave for such false recognition and lose your peace of mind if the world does not praise you? Believe in yourself. People's praises do not last long and are not worth it. Do your duty ethically and sincerely and leave the rest to God.

4. Do not be jealous: We have all experienced how jealousy can disturb our peace of mind. You know you work harder than your colleagues in office but they get all the promotions and you do not. You started a business several years ago but you are not as successful as your neighbor whose business is only one year old. There are several such examples in every walk of life. Should you be jealous? No! Remember that everybody's life is shaped by his previous karma, which has now become his destiny. If you are destined to be rich, the world cannot stop you. If you are not destined to be so, no one can help you to. Nothing can be gained by blaming others for your misfortune. Jealousy will not get you anywhere, but will only give you restlessness.

5. Change yourself according to the environment: If you try to change the environment single-handedly, the chances are you may fail. Instead, change yourself to suit the environment. As you do this, even the environment, which has remained unfriendly to you, will mysteriously appear to be congenial and harmonious.

6. Endure what cannot be cured: This is the best way to turn a disadvantage into an advantage. Every day we face numerous inconveniences, ailments, irritations and accidents that are beyond our control. We must learn to put up with these things. We must learn to endure them cheerfully. Think that everything is God's will. God's logic is beyond our comprehension. When you believe this, you will gain patience, inner strength, and willpower.

7. Do not bite more than you can chew: This maxim should always be remembered. We often tend to take on more responsibilities than we can carry out. This is done to satisfy our ego. Know your limitations. Why should you take on additional load that may create more worries? You cannot gain peace of mind by expanding your external activities. If you have extra time, then spend it in an inward life of prayer, introspection, and meditation. This will reduce unnecessary thoughts in your mind, which make you restless. Fewer the thoughts, greater is the peace of mind.

8. Meditate regularly: Meditation makes the mind clear. It brings the highest state of peace of mind. Try and experience it. If you meditate earnestly for half an hour every day, you will tend to become calm during the remaining twenty-three-and-a-half hours. Your mind will not be disturbed as much as before. You must gradually increase the period of meditation every day. You may think this will interfere with your daily work. On the contrary, this will increase your efficiency and you will produce more work in less time.

9. Never leave the mind vacant: An empty mind is a devil's workshop. All evil deeds start in the mind. Keep your mind occupied in something positive, something worthwhile. Actively follow a hobby. Do something that holds your interest. You must decide what you value more—money or peace of mind. Your hobby may not always earn you money, but you will have a sense of fulfillment and achievement. Even if you are resting, occupy yourself in healthy reading or mental chanting of God's name (*japa*).

10. Do not procrastinate and never regret: Do not waste time wondering 'should I or shouldn't I?' Days, weeks, months and years may be wasted in this futile mental debating. You can never plan enough because you can never anticipate all future happenings. Always remember that God has His own plan too. Value your time and do things accordingly. It does not matter if you fail the first time. You can rectify your mistakes and succeed the next time. Sitting back and worrying will lead to nothing. Learn from your mistakes, but do not brood over the past. Do not regret! Whatever happened was destined to happen. Look at it as the will of God. You do not have the power to alter the course of God's will. So, why cry over spilt milk?

ॐ

Three Ways to Deal with Jealousy

What is good and what is bad?
Fools cannot see at all.
With a garment tied to its tail,
Can the rat enter its hole?
~ Sant Kabir (1398-1448)

Sant Kabir says that foolish people cannot discriminate between good and evil. Such men cannot be happy because the load of evil becomes too heavy for them. Jealousy is one of the unnecessary evils we burden ourselves with. None of us can honestly say that we have not been jealous of more fortunate ones ever.

Ironically, jealousy is generally found among equals or near equals, like friends of equal social status, colleagues in the office, and relatives.

We are not jealous of someone who is too highly placed or is too distantly connected with us. How many of us care about who becomes the President of the US or the Prime Minister of India!

Jealousy keeps us discouraged, frustrated, and disappointed. It makes us gloomy. It is such a depressing feeling that we can neither reveal it to our best friends nor contain it within ourselves. Consequently, it leaves us with a peculiar kind of misery. If this is allowed to grow unchecked beyond a limit, it works like a slow poison to our healthy nature.

The question is this: how do you annihilate this undesirable evil? The following three suggestions may help.

1. Stop comparing yourself with others. Comparisons are always harmful. If they are in your favor, they bring false pride in you. If they are against you, they depress you. Pride can make you overconfident and eventually can be the cause of your downfall.

Jealousy can make you lose self-reliance and force you to seek unjust methods to put down your friend, colleague, or relative. And ultimately you end up with frustration. So, to bring jealousy under control, avoid comparing yourself with others as much as possible. Think that you are unique because that is how God wanted you to be. Pursue in all seriousness your own ideal, whatever it is. Do not waste your precious time in idle and miserable envy.

2. Have patience and wait. No one is lucky or unlucky every time in life. Work hard and wait for your lucky days when good fortune embraces you and others look up to you with envy. This may sound like a defensive strategy and a doubtful method. But use this waiting period to drive jealousy out of your mind. Thus, you can turn a defensive strategy of biding your time into a positive blessing. And then the possibilities are limitless.

3. Let everyone be happy. You have wished for world peace and happiness whenever you prayed. It is about time you practiced it. It is a golden principle to be adopted in order to rise above petty jealousy. Think that you and the others, who are just fragments of the universal soul, are the fingers of the same palm. No jealousy exists among the fingers, in spite of the differences in their lengths. If your child is more intelligent than you, you are not jealous of him or her. Are you? Why? Think! It is because you love your child. Can't you love others the same way? If your friend, colleague, or relative is enjoying a few advantages over you now, be happy for him or her. Surely your turn will come too. Full justice is meted out to every individual soul in the long run. This is the divine law. Have faith and adopt this spirit in action.

How to Keep Pride, Ego, and Arrogance at Bay

Hypocrisy, pride, self-conceit, wrath, arrogance and ignorance belong to him who is born to the heritage of the demons.
~ *The Gita, XVI - 4*

Why do I wish to talk about pride and arrogance? Because in my opinion, while pride harms only the proud man, arrogance due to overbearing pride brings contempt for others too. An arrogant man is often rude and very fond of offending his friends, relatives, colleagues and everyone else who meets him.

Pride

Pride rears its head even in the most unsuspected corner. One man may be proud that he is proud, and another person may be proud that he is not proud. While one may be proud that he is a non-believer in God, another may be proud of his devotion to God. Learning may render one man proud; ignorance can also be the source of pride for another man.

Ego

Ego is nothing but pride in an inflated form. For example, an arrogant man is unduly and excessively proud of his wealth, status and learning. He shows ego in spirit of conduct. He is unjustifiably overbearing and haughty. His head is swollen like the swelling caused by dropsy. He thinks very highly of himself and poorly of others. He claims a lot about himself and concedes very little to others.

Arrogance

Arrogance is an absorbing sense of one's own greatness. It is a feeling of one's superiority over the others. In the presence of superiors, overweening pride manifests itself as arrogance and one is too involved with oneself to care to see the good in others and praise them.

Vanity

Another byproduct of pride is vanity, which intensely craves admiration and applause. It is undue assumption of self-importance. It often results in open and rude expression of contempt and hostility. It quickly takes for granted superiority and privilege, which others are slow to concede.

Why is it Difficult to Ward Off Ego?

If you think pride or ego is easy to get rid of, think again! The play of ego pervades our entire life. Ego does not go away by merely substituting 'I' with another phrase. As long as the body is alive and the mind functions inside and through the body, what is known as the ego or the personality will raise its head and exist. This ego or pride is not a permanent and unquestionable reality. It is a temporary phenomenon; it is ignorance that invests itself with permanency. Ego is a concept; it is ignorance that elevates it to the status of reality. Only enlightenment can bring you this wisdom.

The Underlying Paradox

How does enlightenment arise? How does the realization that God is the real doer and we are just His means get instilled in our hearts? I am sure you will agree that until this realization arises in our minds and inner intelligence, we cannot get rid of our ego. One may very easily say, "Practice *Karma Yoga* (see article on *Karma Yoga*) and the ego will disappear." Is practicing *Karma Yoga* as simple it sounds? For instance, if you say that you have been a *karmayogi* who does his duty and does not look for rewards, for several years, then you become so vain and arrogant that the ego waxes gloriously inside you, instead of getting eliminated. The argument is that if you are established in the practice of *karma yoga*, your heart is purified; and then in that pure heart divine grace dispels the darkness of the ego. Possibly! But before you get to that stage, the ego becomes so great that the earlier philosophy is completely forgotten.

May God Bless You!

So, what should we do to exorcise the devil of pride (ego) and arrogance? In my opinion, only by the grace of God can one be watchful of the presence of pride in all actions. How does one earn God's grace? You cannot earn it because that will again involve your ego.

In the Gita, Lord Krishna says, "On account of pure compassion, I bestow knowledge on my devotee. I give it out of compassion, not because he deserves it." Mark the Lord's words. He says, "My devotee." Who is His devotee? He whose heart all the time cries, "My God, what am I going to do? I can't get rid of my ego. I cannot deal with my pride" is a devotee. The devotee hopes that one day, by the miraculous grace of God, someone, probably a guru (spiritual master), would come into his or her life, switch on enlightenment, and put off his or her pride. Until then, all that the devotee can do is to keep praying.

Ten Commandments for a Successful Married Life

What does it take to be an ideal spouse? Here are some tried and tested means to keep your married life sound, peaceful and free from conjugal tension.

1. Love comes first: Physical love is good, but there must be genuine spiritual love in your heart. Your immediate neighbor is your own spouse. So, let charity begin at home. Set an example by loving your spouse first and foremost of all people. Follow the scripture 'love thy neighbor as thyself'.

2. Narrow the gulf: Whether it is a love marriage, arranged marriage, or a forced marriage, differences are bound to arise. Both of you (the husband and the wife) come from different backgrounds, upbringing and environment. You must be ready to overlook the differences, lapses and shortcomings.

3. Forgive and forget: Remember that to forgive is divine. Keep doing it, even if you need to repeat this process an infinite number of times.

4. Begin the day in a cool manner: Early in the morning, both the spouses should try to remain calm and cool. There must be no discussions or arguments in the early hours of the day.

5. Silence can save: When you leave home for work in the morning, be at your best behavior. If one of you is provoked or complains about something, silence is the best answer. Conversely, you can say, "We will discuss it in the evening."

6. Inquire and appreciate: After you return home, enquire and take interest in each other's activities during the day. "How was your day?" is a soothing question that does wonders. You must show your genuine appreciation and sympathy. Top it with a pleasant smile.

7. Listen and sympathize: Do listen to your spouse attentively and sympathetically. Never ignore his or her concerns. Even at your place of work, if you get a telephone call from your partner, be polite and courteous, in spite of your busy schedule.

8. Don't forget to compliment: Make use of words and phrases like 'thank you', 'well done', 'you have done a good job', and 'I am sorry' as frequently as is necessary. Be generous in your praise and compliments.

9. Don't compare: Do not enter into comparisons. No one is 100 per cent perfect or 100 per cent imperfect. We all have flaws and shortcomings. Always look at the good qualities of your spouse.

10. Keep smiling: Be cheerful and smile away your problems. Give a smile as often as you can. Only a human being is endowed with this blessing. Animals do not have this rare faculty. Did you know that you use only twenty muscles for a smile but seventy muscles are expended for a frown? So, keep smiling!

Ideals of a Hindu Marriage

In Hinduism, the man and the woman represent two halves of the divine body. There is no question of superiority or inferiority between them. However, it is a scientific fact that the emotional side is more developed in women. This does not mean that intellectually women are inferior. Hindu history is replete with examples of superwomen like Gargi, Maitreyi and Sulabha, whose faculty of reasoning was far superior to that of ordinary mortals. But owing to organic differences in physical and emotional constitutions, women are temperamentally more emotional than men.

The Idea of Marriage

The idea behind the institution of marriage in Hinduism is to foster love for the entire family. Self-interest is not a focus in marriage. Practice of self-restraint is also one of the ideals of marriage in Hinduism. Love and duty for the entire family prevents break-ups and breakdowns in a marriage.

Men by nature are less capable of self-restraint than women. That is why after marriage the Hindu women lead the men by keeping the lustful propensity under control. The thoughts of any other man do not enter the mind of a Hindu married woman until she loses her faith in her husband due to his consistent misbehavior and 'don't care' attitude.

The Sanctity of Marriage

During the nuptial ceremony in a Vedic marriage, both the bride and the bridegroom take the oath to practice self-restraint, work together for the welfare of the family and help each other attain spiritual peace. These profound ideals of sanctity are a great gift of Hinduism to the world at large.

Protecting the Institution

It is a concern that we have begun to ignore the ancient and profound ideals of Hindu marriage. Consequently, the number of divorce suits filed by Hindu couples is on the rise today. Instead of strengthening the traditional ideals, which for thousands of years have helped us prevent break-ups and breakdowns, we are misdirecting our energies towards promoting the ideal of sense-enjoyment and self-interest. It is still not too late to be proactive in protecting the sanctity of Hindu marriage.

How to Approach Death

"Death is not extinguishing the light; it is putting out the lamp because dawn has come."
~ **Rabindranath Tagore**

As we grow old, we often begin to think of life after death. The fear of death is founded upon the love of life, which is the deepest instinct in human nature. We are talking about death as a natural phenomenon. Death that makes its presence felt through disease and old age is distinct from death due to accidents and natural calamities, for the latter is a totally different directive process.

The Fear Factor

Let us first accept the fact that most of us loathe death because of the uncertainty of its time and place. Failure to survive when the time comes is the basic fear. The unwillingness to face this fear with proper understanding is due to the emphasis we lay upon the physical body. It is also based upon an innate fear of loneliness due to the loss of those we have been familiar with during our worldly existence.

Loneliness After Death

The thought of loneliness after death establishes the fact that there is life after death. Simply put, there are now many evidences in favor of the existence of soul consciousness after death, based on several anecdotes on out-of-body experiences.

Francis Bacon has said in one of his aphorisms: "It is as natural to die as to be born; and to a little infant, perhaps, the one is as painful as the other." Yet, loneliness after death is nothing as compared to loneliness at birth. At birth, the soul finds itself in new surroundings and in a body that is at first totally incompetent to take care of itself or establish intelligent contact with the surrounding conditions for a long period of time. The child at birth has relationship with the family members. This loneliness disappears gradually as they come in contact with those who are congenial to them and eventually become their friends and family.

Afterlife Consciousness

After death, there is no loneliness as the dead find the people they knew while they were alive in the physical plane. They may be one's parents, relatives, or friends who had died before them. After death, the person is also conscious of the friends and family members who are still alive. The dead can see them, and can tune into their emotions and thinking too.

Can We Welcome Death?

One must accept the fact that consciousness remains the same whether it is in the physical body or outside it. This consciousness develops with great ease when it is not limited and conditioned by the brain consciousness in the physical body. Death releases the individual life into a less cramped and confined existence. Therefore, one need not fear death or anything that lies beyond it. In fact, one should welcome death, because one would be making a transition into a higher plane of consciousness. Freedom from the limitations of the physical body is a real beneficence.

Let the Soul Live on...

The *Bhagavad Gita* talks about the eternal soul and the necessity for the soul to live spiritually, constructively and divinely within the physical body. So, why not make our physical existence as pleasant as possible for others, so that they will remember us for years later? What do we have to lose?

Become Soul-conscious

We brought nothing with us when we came into this world and we would take nothing with us when we leave this world. In fact, we all leave a little extra behind if we lead a life of goodness and philanthropy. If we become soul-conscious, death will be an 'ordered' process, carried out in full consciousness and with understanding of the cyclic purpose of birth and death.

Once this is understood, the fear of death ceases to exist. It gives us power to control our passing over to the other side of the veil. Let us approach death with as much normalcy as we can muster.

Karma and Free Will

Although *karma* literally means deed or act, the doctrine or law of karma and the word 'karma' have become synonymous in the western world. In other words, karma is broadly accepted as the principle of cause and effect, akin to the law of action and reaction (Newton's Third Law of Motion that states that for every action there is an equal and opposite reaction). The law of karma states that every mental, emotional and physical act, no matter how insignificant it is, eventually returns to the individual with equal impact.

Categories of Karma

There are three categories of karma:

1. *Sanchita Karma* – the sum total of past karma yet to bear fruit.

2. *Prarabdha Karma* – that portion of *sanchita karma* that shows its effect in the present

3. *Kriyamana Karma* – this is the karma that one is creating at present; it will determine his or her tomorrow

Relationship between Karma and Free Will

The negative karma of the past can be softened, if not totally eliminated, by creating positive karma in the present. This brings us to the relationship between karma and free will. One of the three categories of karma cited above—the *prarabdha karma*, which is the part of one's past karma bearing fruit in the present of the individual—has two components: fixed and variable. The fixed component of the *prarabdha karma* is beyond one's control and it consists of that component of the past karma in one's previous lives. This determines your parents, how you look – the general features of your body, and the place and environment you are born in. The variable component of *prarabdha karma* remains latent in the child in the form of natural habits and tendencies. The variable component can be overcome by one's initiative and free will. Remember, you cannot change your parents, how you look or your place of birth, but by the power of your individual will you can alter the effects of the variable component of the *prarabdha karma* and achieve success in any endeavor.

The Equation

Author Bansi Pandit in his book *The Hindu Mind* proposes the following equation to explain karma and free will:

Success (S) = Effort (E) x *Prarabdha* or Destiny (D)

Here, the fixed portion of *prarabdha karma* has been translated to destiny because it refers to that component of the past karma that already has begun to bear the fruit and nothing can be done about it.

In the above equation, S can range from 0 to 1. When S equals zero, there is zero success or complete failure. When S is equal to 1, there is 100 per cent success. Likewise, E ranges from 0 to 1. When E equals zero, there is zero or no effort. When E equals 1, there is 100 per cent effort. Similarly, D also ranges from 0 to 1. If D equals zero, there is only past bad karma. If D equals 1, there is good fortune or good karma.

Now look at the equation again. S = E x D. If D is 1 and E is zero, S will be zero. This means, even with the best destiny due to one's past best karma, success is directly proportional to one's efforts and your free will to work hard or not. Thus, the only way S can be equal to 1 is by having both D (destiny) and E (individual effort) equal to 1. Therefore, it can be concluded logically that destiny or *prarabdha karma* alone cannot lead to success unless effort is maximized.

Again, from the equation of success, it follows that if D is equal to zero, S will be zero, even if E equals 1. This is the power of one's predetermined destiny. Pandit therefore concludes, "Since a person's destiny in the present life is based on his karma from previous incarnations, he has no control of the impact of his predetermined destiny on his present life. All he can do is maximize his effort in the present life. Although the impact of an individual's destiny cannot be underestimated, it is the effort that he must control by utilizing his free will. On a broader level, this means that one must do the best one can and not worry about the results."

Glory of the Guru

The word 'guru' can be applied to three different sets of people: 1. Parent: the instiller of *sanskaras* or moral and cultural values; 2. Teacher: the one who teaches worldly knowledge; 3. Spiritual master: the one who gives us spiritual enlightenment. Here, we will dwell upon the guru as a spiritual master.

Why We Need a Guru

The word 'guru' is made up of two Sanskrit root words namely '*gu*', which means 'darkness' or 'ignorance', and '*ru*', which means 'dispeller'. Thus 'guru' means the dispeller of darkness or ignorance. In essence, the guru is the perfect spiritual master, the ideal saint and the faultless guide with realized wisdom, who dispels ignorance and liberates his disciples from the bondage of mundane pleasures.

You may wonder why reading scriptures cannot dispel ignorance. Swami Shivananda has answered this question in the following quotation: "The scriptures are like a forest. There are ambiguous passages. There are passages that are apparently contradictory. There are passages that have esoteric meanings, diverse significance, and hidden explanations. There are cross-references. You are in need of a guru or preceptor who will explain to you the right meaning, who will remove doubts and ambiguities, who will place before you the essence of the teachings."

Some read the Gita, Bhagavatam and Ramayana for a few years and still remain ignorant and restless. Then they begin to search for a guru. It is through the guru that one comes to realize God and is unshackled from the fetters of material bondage. So, the guru occupies a prime place in Hindu spirituality.

How to Find an Appropriate Guru

Although a guru is necessary for every aspirant in the spiritual path, one must be extremely careful before accepting any preacher as his or her guru. These days there is a flood of gurus. These self-proclaimed gurus whisper a mantra into an individual's ear and stretch their hand for money. Such people are not fit to be called gurus. Today, there are many good disciples, but it is very difficult to find a true guru.

Veda Vyasa says: "One desirous of knowing the highest good should resort to a preceptor, who is well-versed in the implication of the Vedas, has realized *para brahman* and who is free from attachment and hatred."

Swami Shivananda again says, "If you find peace in the presence of a *mahatma* (great soul), if you are inspired by his speeches, if he is able to clear your doubts, if he is free from greed, anger, and lust, if he is selfless, loving, and I-less, you can take him as your guru. He who is able to clear your doubts, he who is sympathetic in your *sadhana*, he who does not disturb your beliefs but helps you from where you are, in whose very presence you feel spiritually elevated, he is your guru. Once you choose your guru, implicitly follow him. God will guide you through the guru."

Who is a Sadguru?

A *sadguru* possesses all the qualities of a true guru described earlier. However, what sets a *sadguru* apart from the other gurus are his possession of countless *siddhis* or psychic and divine powers of an incarnation. Even when he is not preaching, his presence or company is elevating, inspiring and illuminating.

Our scriptures say: "*Gurur Brahma, Gurur Vishnu, Guru Devo Maheshwara; Guru Sakshat Param Brahma, tasmai Shri guruve namaha.*" This means the guru is Brahma, the guru is Vishnu, and the guru is Shiva. Clearly, the guru is the supreme Brahman; to that *sadguru* we salute.

Sant Kabir said: "If all the land were turned to paper and all the seas turned to ink, and all the forests into pens to write with, they would still not suffice to describe the greatness of the *sadguru.*"

In sum, one needs a true guru to help reveal the esoteric truths hidden in the scriptures.

V
Prayer Power

How prayers can help us find our way in life

The Importance of Devotion

The *Bhagavad Gita*, the greatest and holiest of Hindu scriptures, emphasizes the importance of *bhakti* or loving devotion to God. *Bhakti*, the Gita says, is the only way to realize God.

In Chapter 2, *shloka* (verse) 7, Arjuna asks, "My soul is oppressed by a sense of frustration. My mind is unable to determine what is right. I am requesting you to tell me definitely what is for my good. I am your pupil. Teach me. I have surrendered myself to you."

Krishna does not answer Arjuna until Chapter 18, *shlokas* 65-66 where He says, "Let your mind be constantly directed towards me; be devoted to me; dedicate all your actions to me; prostrate before me; over and above the claims of all *dharma* (duties) completely surrender to me and me alone."

However, Krishna does partially answer Arjuna in Chapter 11, *shlokas* 53-55 after exhibiting His cosmic form, "It is not possible to see me as you have done through the study of the Vedas or by austerities or gifts or by sacrifice; it is only by one-pointed devotion (*bhakti*) to me and me alone that you see and know me as I am in reality, and ultimately reach me. He who dedicates all his notions and actions to me with a knowledge of my superiority, he who is my devotee with no attachment, and he who has no enmity to any living being can reach me."

Bhakti therefore, is the only way to the true knowledge of God and the surest way to reach Him.

Bhakti: Unwavering Devotion and Love for God

Bhakti, according to the Gita, is the love for God and love

reinforced by a true knowledge of the glory of God. It surpasses the love for all worldly things. This love is constant and is centered in God and God alone, and cannot be shaken under any circumstances, whether in prosperity or in adversity.

Bhakti is not for everyone. All human beings fall into two categories, the devotees (*bhaktas*) and the non-devotees (*abhaktas*). Lord Krishna says that the Gita is not for the *abhaktas*.

In Chapter 18, *shloka* 67, Krishna says, "This (Gita) is not to be communicated to one who is not disciplined, is not a devotee, has not served the learned or hates me." He also says in Chapter 7, *shlokas* 15 and 16: "The lowest among men, those of wicked deeds, and the foolish ones, do not resort to me; for their mind is overcome by *maya* (illusion) and their nature is *asuri* (demonic), inclined to worldly pleasures. Four kinds of people of good deeds turn to me—those who are in distress, who search for knowledge, who desire worldly good deeds or who are truly wise." The Lord further elaborates in the 28th *shloka* of the same chapter: "It is only those of good deeds whose sins are ended, and who are freed from the spell of opposites that run to me with firm determination."

Who is an ideal devotee?

Even those with *bhakti* must have certain qualities to gain the grace of God. This is explained in detail in Chapter 12, *shlokas* 13-20 of the Gita. The ideal devotee (*bhakta*) should...

- not hate any living being
- cultivate friendship and compassion
- give up the feeling of 'I' and 'mine'
- be unmoved by happiness or misery
- be forgiving
- strive for self-control
- always be content with what s/he has
- have a strong determination
- surrender his/her mind and intellect to God
- not be afraid of anyone, and none in the world should fear him/her
- desire nothing
- be pure and efficient
- be free from elation, anger, fear and turbulence of mind

- be indifferent to what befalls him/her
- be free from weakness of mind
- be free from the feeling that s/he is an independent agent
- have no feeling of elation and enmity or desire
- develop an attitude of mind that rejects good as well as bad things
- have no attachments and should accept pain and pleasure, honor and disgrace, heat and cold equally as his/her portion
- look upon friends and foes alike
- not indulge in idle talk
- not get attached to any fixed abode
- be steadfast in mind

A *bhakta* who is all of the above is dear to Krishna. Most important of all, the *bhaktas* who love Him with full faith in his supremacy are most dear to God. May we all be worthy of Gita's *bhakti*.

Power of Mantra Chanting

Mananaat traayate iti mantrah
(That which uplifts by constant repetition is a mantra.)

Hindus believe that mantras can lift the believer towards a higher self. These sound elements of Sanskrit language are permanent entities and are of everlasting significance. In the recitation of Sanskrit mantras, the sound is very important, for it can bring transformation in you while leading you to power and strength.

The Significance of Sound

Different sounds have different effects on the human psyche. The soft sound of wind rustling through leaves soothes our nerves, while the musical note of a running stream enchants our heart. Thunder may cause awe and fear.

The sacred utterances or chanting of Sanskrit mantras provide us the power to attain our goals and lift ourselves from the ordinary to the higher level of consciousness. They give us the power to cure diseases, ward off evil, gain wealth, acquire supernatural powers, worship a deity for exalted communion, achieve a blissful state and attain liberation.

The Origin of Mantras

The teachings of the Vedas consist of various mantras and hymns cognized by different seers or *rishis* from the cosmic mind. As the Vedas are impersonal and eternal, the exact historical date of the origin of mantra chanting is hard to arrive at. For example, every mantra in the Vedas, Upanishads and religious traditions (*sampradaya*) within the Hindu religion begin with *Om* or *Aum*, which is a primordial sound that is said to have originated at the time of the creation of the cosmos also referred to as the Big Bang.

Om: The Beginning and the End

The Bible (John 1:1) says: "In the beginning was the word and the word was with God and the word was God." Modern Vedic philosophers have interpreted this teaching of the Bible and equated *Om* or *Aum* with God. *Om* or *Aum* is the most important of all mantras. All mantras generally begin and often also end with *Om*.

Healing by Mantropathy

The chanting of *Om* in transcendental meditation has now received widespread recognition. Mantras can be used to treat tension and many other ailments. The Brahmvarchas Shodh Sansthan, a research center for integration of science and spirituality in Shantikunj, Haridwar, India undertakes extensive experiments on *mantra shakti* or the power of mantras. The result of these experiments is used to testify that mantropathy can be used scientifically for healing and environment cleansing.

How to Chant the Mantras

There are many schools of thought on the methods of chanting. A mantra chanted correctly or incorrectly, knowingly or unknowingly, carefully or carelessly, is sure to bear the desired result for physical and mental wellbeing. It is also believed by many that the glory of mantra chanting cannot be established through reasoning and intellect. It can only be experienced and realized through devotion, faith and constant repetition of the mantra.

According to some Vedic scholars, mantra chanting is 'mantra yoga'. The simple yet powerful mantra *Om* or *Aum* harmonizes the physical forces with the emotional and intellectual forces. When this happens, you begin to feel like a complete being, mentally and physically. But this process is very slow and requires a lot of patience and unfailing faith.

The Guru Mantra

Healing through chanting can be expedited if the mantra is received from a guru. A guru adds a divine potency to the mantra. It becomes more effective and thus helps the chanter in heal faster.

Keep the Faith

It is important to have complete faith in the recitation of mantras. It is primarily through faith, aided by strong will, that one achieves one's goals. A sound body and a calm mind are essential while chanting mantras. Once you are free from all worries and have achieved stability in mind and body, you will derive maximum benefit through the recitation of mantras. You must have a definite object in view and a strong willpower to obtain the desired objective. You must then direct the will to achieve your goal.

The Gayatri Mantra: Giver of Righteous Wisdom

The Gayatri mantra is one of the oldest and most powerful of Sanskrit mantras. It is believed that by chanting the Gayatri mantra and firmly establishing it in the mind, and by carrying out the task ordained for you, your life will be full of happiness.

The word 'Gayatri' itself explains the reason for the existence of this mantra. It has its origin in the Sanskrit phrase *Gayantam triyate iti*; the phrase refers to that mantra which rescues the chanter from all adverse situations that may lead to mortality.

Goddess Gayatri is also called 'Veda Mata' or the Mother of Vedas – the reality behind the experienced and cognized universe.

The meter in the Gayatri mantra consists of 24 syllables, generally arranged in a triplet of eight syllables each. Therefore, the meter (*tripadhi*) is also known as the Gayatri meter or the Gayatri *chhanda*.

The Mantra

Aum
Bhur Bhuvah Svah
Tat Savitur Varenyam
Bhargo Devasya Dheemahi
Dhiyo Yo nah Prachodayat
~ The Rig Veda (10:16:3)

The Meaning

O thou existence, absolute, creator of the three dimensions, we contemplate upon thy divine light. May He stimulate our intellect and bestow upon us true knowledge.

Or simply,

O Divine mother, our hearts are filled with darkness. Please make this darkness distant from us and promote illumination within us.

Let us take each word of the Gayatri mantra and try to understand its inherent meaning.

The First Word *Om (Aum)*

It is also called *pranav* because the sound emanates from the *prana* or the vital vibration, which feels the universe. The scripture says, "*Aum iti ek akshara Brahman* (The one syllable *Aum* is *Brahman*).

What happens when you pronounce *Aum*? A emerges from the throat, originating in the region of the navel; U rolls over the tongue; M ends on the lips; A refers to waking, U is dreaming and M is sleeping. It is the sum and substance of all the words that can emanate from the human throat. It is the primordial fundamental sound symbolic of the Universal Absolute.

The *Vyahrities: Bhuh, Bhuvah and Svah*

The above three words of the Gayatri are called *vyahrities*. *Vyahriti* is that which gives knowledge of the entire cosmos or *ahriti*. The scripture says, "*Visheshenh Aahritih sarva viraat, praahlaanam prakashokaranh vyahritih.*"

Now, let us understand the different meanings of these words given in the scriptures:

Bhuh	Bhuvah	Svah
Earth	Atmosphere	Beyond atmosphere
Past	Present	Future
Morning	Noon	Evening
Tamas	Rajas	Sattwa
Gross	Subtle	Causal

Thus, by uttering these three words, the chanter contemplates the glory of God that illumines the three worlds or the regions of experience.

The Remaining Words of the Gayatri Mantra

Tat simply means 'that' because it defies description through speech or language; it is the Ultimate Reality. *Savitur* means 'Divine Sun' (the ultimate light of wisdom) not to be confused with the ordinary sun. *Varenium* means 'adore.' *Bhargo* means 'illumination.' *Devasya* means 'Divine Grace.' *Dheemahi* means 'we contemplate.' *Dhi* means 'intellect.' *Yo* means 'who.' *Nah* means 'ours.' *Prachodayat* means 'requesting / urging / praying.'

The above words constitute the prayer for final liberation through the awakening of our true intelligence. The inherent meaning of the prayer is: May we receive God's supreme sin-destroying light, which will guide our intellect in the right direction.

The Vedic scholars selected the words of the Gayatri mantra and arranged them so that they not only conveyed meaning but also created a specific power of righteous wisdom through their utterance. All the problems of a person are solved if s/he is endowed with the gift of righteous wisdom. Righteous wisdom starts emerging soon after *japa* or recitation of the Gayatri mantra.

Why and How to Pray

If you are confused about the underlying philosophy of prayer because your prayers are seldom answered, the following insights into the success of prayers may help you.

Twelve Reasons to Pray

To begin with, here's why we generally pray:

1. We pray to God for help in distress.
2. We pray asking God for enlightenment.
3. We pray for communion with God through single-minded devotion.
4. We pray asking for peace from God when the mind is restless.
5. We pray to surrender ourselves to God completely.
6. We pray to God for giving us the ability to comfort others.
7. We pray thanking God for His blessings.
8. We pray expecting God to decide what is best for us when we are in a dilemma.
9. We pray for friendship with God.
10. We pray for melting the mind and ego.
11. We pray requesting God to give us strength, peace and pure intellect, through the Gayatri mantra, for instance.
12. We pray asking God to purify the heart and make us abide by Him forever.

Two Parts of a Prayer

Essentially, what the above 12 reasons convey to us is that a prayer has two parts: one is soliciting a favor from the Almighty and the other is surrendering ourselves to His will. While the first part is practiced by most of us daily, the second part is the real goal because it implies dedication. Dedication means feeling the light of God within your heart. If your heart is devoid of divine light, you will not be happy, cheerful and successful in your lives.

Guard Your Selfish Desires

We must remember that your success depends on the inward state of your mind. Your mind will create hindrance in your work if it is not in communion with God because He alone is the permanent abode of peace.

Most of us want to be healthy, wealthy and wise. But if we always approached God with a begging attitude, we are treating Him as our bearer to supply the things required by us at once. This is no devotion to God but devotion to our own selfish desires.

The scriptures indicate that there are seven techniques of successful prayer:

1. When you pray just talk to God as a little boy would to a father or mother whom he loves and with whom he feels in harmony. Tell Him everything that is on your mind and in your heart.

2. Talk to God in simple everyday speech. He understands every language. It is not necessary to use an exaggerated formal speech. You would not talk to your father or mother that way, would you? God is your heavenly father (or mother). Why should you be formal to Him or Her? This will make your relationship with Him more natural.

3. Tell God what you want. You might as well be factual. You want something. Tell Him about it. Tell Him you would like to have it if He thinks it is good for you. But also say and mean it that you will leave it to Him to decide and you will accept His decision as best for you. If you do this regularly it will bring to you what you ought to have, and thus fulfill your own destiny. It will be possible for God to give you things that you should have wonderful things. It is really unfortunate, the marvelous things we miss, things God wants to give us and cannot because we insist upon something else, something only a fraction as fine as He wants to give us.

4. Practice praying as many times during the day as possible. Most importantly say a little prayer before you go to bed. If it is not possible, get into bed, relax and then pray. God will lull you to a wonderful carefree sleep.

5. It is not always necessary to say words when you pray. Spend a few moments just thinking about Him. Think how good He is, how kind He is, and that He is right by your side guiding and watching over you.

6. Don't always pray for yourself. Try helping others by your prayers. Pray for those who are in trouble or are ill. Whether they are your loved ones or your friends or neighbors, your prayer will profoundly affect them. And...

7. Last but not the least, whatever you do, do not make all prayers into the form of begging God for something. The prayer for thanksgiving is much more powerful. Make your prayer consisting of a listing of all the fine things you possess or all the wonderful things that have happened to you. Name them over, thank God for them and make that your whole prayer. You will find that these prayers of thanksgiving grow.

Finally, please do not pray to God to run after you to satisfy your selfish desires. You are supposed to do your work as efficiently and skillfully as possible. With faith in God and using the above techniques of prayer, you will have success in every walk of life.

The Yoga of Kirtan

The Sanskrit word 'yoga' is derived from the root verb 'yuj', which means 'union'. The supreme union of the individual mind and the cosmic mind is yoga. 'Kirtan' literally means chanting the divine names.

In his *Yogasutras*, Patanjali advocated the eight-fold path of Astanga Yoga. The eight limbs are: *yama* (self-restraint), *niyama* (life-regulating moral rules and observances), *asana* (postures of bodily restfulness), *pranayama* (breath control), *pratyahara* (withdrawal of senses), *dharana* (fixing the mind on the Supreme), *dhyana* (absorption of self), and *samadhi* (liberation of the soul). These eight branches are closely related to every aspect of human life. Contrary to popular perception, *asana* is only one aspect of yoga; it does not represent yoga comprehensively. In its entirety, yoga is a well-knit, disciplined science of attaining supreme bliss.

Kirtan and Astanga Yoga

Kirtan brings about almost the same results as Astanga Yoga. Kirtan is sung in a group comprising devotees, with a lead singer. The fixed tunes, repetition of words and phrases lend a kind of tonal mesmerism. Anecdotes, episodes from the lives of Gods, preaching of saints and description of God's glories are generally the subjects of Kirtan. The importance and efficacy of Kirtan have been dealt with at some length not only by the Hindu scriptures but also by the scriptures of other religions. The sages and saints of India have sung passionately about the greatness and glory of divine names, thus creating devotional literature both in Sanskrit and regional languages. Their exquisite beauty is unsurpassed by any other religious literature of the world. Therefore, to think that divine names are chanted only by the idle and indolent people and simpletons is a sign of great misfortune and ignorance.

Can Patanjali's Astanga Yoga be accomplished through Kirtan? Yes. While fervently chanting divine names, or listening to the Kirtan of other devotees, a devotee becomes oblivious to his sense organs, thus affecting an easy and imperceptible restraint upon his senses. This corresponds to the first *anga* of Patanjali—*yama*.

Certain radiant energy is inherent in the divine names of God and therefore the vibrations released as a result of regular chanting oxidize or destroy the impurities – both corporal as well as mental – of the devotee, thus developing puritan qualities such as compassion and contentment. This corresponds to the second *anga* of Patanjali—*niyama*.

The wavering of the mind is then arrested and the devotee becomes serene and steady. This forms the third *anga* of Patanjali. The devotee then continues singing; he is suddenly overwhelmed with deep love for his Lord. Tears trickle from their eyes, the voice stutters, the throat is choked with emotion, and the breath stops—thus bringing about *Kevala Kumbhak*, one of the operations in *pranayama* or the fourth *anga* of Patanjali.

There comes a stage in the devotee's onward march when s/he becomes completely absorbed in the Lord's name. As a result, all external objects are shut out from them. This corresponds to *pratyahara*, the fifth *anga* of Patanjali.

The divine name becomes their very breath. This means their speech has merged into their mind and the mind into *prana*, the vital breath. This is *dharana*, the sixth *anga* of Patanjali.

The vital breath dissolves progressively into the fire of his body, thus corresponding to *dhyana* – the seventh *anga* of Patanjali. With the accomplishment of *dhyana*, the Lord appears before him and the devotee remembers only his Lord and excludes all other things. He experiences indescribable and immense bliss – *samadhi*, the eighth *anga* of Patanjali.

Bhakti in the Yoga of Kirtan

Kirtan brings about almost the same results as Patanjali's Astanga Yoga, but in the former the vital conquest is made through *bhakti*, which means intense love for God. When the devotee establishes an identity with their Supreme Lord or deity, they become perfect in their love, which lead them to perfect knowledge and supreme bliss, which are the goals of human existence.

The effects of Kirtan described above are not a fabrication or a fantasy. It is the actual experience of many a saint of India. Sri Chaitanya Mahaprabhu, Namdev, Tukaram, Changdev, Narahari Sonar, Janabai, Muktabai, Mirabai, Surdas and Narsingh Mehta experienced this bliss. These saints achieved through continuous Kirtan what a hatha yogi can achieve by following the system recommended by Patanjali.

The Kirtan of Rama *nama* played a pivotal role in transforming Gandhi to became a Mahatma or a great soul. Kirtan, Gandhi said, gave him power. He became selfless and fearless by getting rid of lust, greed and anger, the foes of the human mind, through Rama *nama* Kirtan.

The greatness and efficacy of Kirtan Yoga cannot be overemphasized. Anyone, irrespective of their religious belief, is competent to follow this divine road to supreme bliss.

The Power of Naam Japa

Naam japa literally means the repetition of God's divine name. The tradition of *japa* in Hinduism dates back to the ancient times of the *rishis*. "Of all the *yajnas*, I am the *japa yajna*," declares Lord Krishna to Arjuna (*Bhagavad Gita, X.2*).

Goswami Tulasidas in *Ramcharitmanas* says, "Through the repetition of God's name, the very ocean of mundane existence gets dried up."

What is the rationale of *japa*? What is its process? Is *japa* without devotion and understanding effective? Let us dwell upon these questions.

Faith in the Divine Name

The genesis of *japa* is based in the ancient perception of sages that the world and all creation proceeds from sound or *Naada Brahman*. There are, however, certain conditions under which *japa* of a divine name produces the intended results. The heart must beat in unison with the name of God. Only then the *japa* gathers strength, acquires a fresh life in the individual and in time begins to repeat itself spontaneously.

Even if complete mental identification and feeling from the heart may not be possible, a strong faith in *naam japa* can be very effective. When repeated with faith for a long time, the divine name keeps creating vibrations in our inner consciousness and gradually the power hidden in the divine name reveals itself in the being. The name is essentially one with the Lord. The name accomplishes everything by its potency and its intrinsic worth. In this age of Kali, there is no means to God-realization other than *naam japa.*

Difference Between Mantra Chanting and *Naam Japa*

For the *mantra* to be effective, it needs to be alive. There is a *chaitanya* or a consciousness in each *mantra,* and that should be awakened. Normally this is done by the guru who gives the *mantra.* He energizes the *mantra* with his spiritual power, sets it alive into motion, and delivers it into the being of the disciple. It is up to the recipient to tend to and nourish the life of the *mantra* received, let it instill itself into the core of his being, and allow it to spread all through his consciousness.

There is no such condition for *naam japa* for it to be effective. Just like how the fire is naturally endowed with the capacity to burn combustible substances, the divine name has the natural capacity to burn away sin. Even reverence is not an essential factor in *naam japa,* though its presence is most welcome. *Naam japa* must be done at all events, even if reverence is lacking.

The wonderful thing about *naam japa* is that there are no stringent regulations regarding its chanting; it can be done by anyone at any time and at any place.

Logic, the Stumbling Block

Logic intervenes and misleads us by arguing that one's hunger is not appeased by merely repeating the word 'bread'. But the divine name is not a material sound like the word 'bread'. The word itself is *Brahman.* There is no distinction between the name and the object signified by it, viz., God. Control of the mind is the most difficult job; an endeavor to silence the mind is a difficult task to undertake. But repeating the divine name is an easy recipe for mind control.

Types of *Naam Japa*

There are three kinds of *naam japa:*

1. *Vaachika:* The divine name is pronounced in a clear, distinct and loud manner.

2. *Upaamsu:* The divine name is pronounced distinctly but in a very low tone so that only the person repeating it knows the name. Only the lips move in this kind of *japa.*

3. *Maanasa* or mental *japa:* Here, there is no movement of any of the vocal organs or the lips.

In the traditional method of *japa,* the number of times a divine name is repeated in a sitting is fixed. The number sometimes has an occult significance. A rosary is generally used to keep count of the number.

The rosary or *japa mala* usually contains 108 beads, of which one is bigger than the rest. The large sized bead is the *meru*. The beads are rolled using the right thumb and the middle finger (of the right hand). The *meru* must not be crossed. When one reaches the *meru*, it means the *japa* has been done 108 times and the fingers must be turned back from the last bead for another 108, and so on. The number of times the *mala* is completed is recorded, usually by moving the left thumb along the three lines of each finger of the left hand.

The *naam japa* is perfected aloud with sincere and faithful practice. Then the *japa* is done with a soft voice. And then it is done mentally. At the mental level, the *japa* is done silently; the sound is perceived mentally without the support of the tongue or any other external limb of the body. This is called a*jappaa japa* (unchanted or silent chant). The ultimate accomplishment is the performance of *naam japa* while walking, standing, sitting, eating, working or sleeping. Internally, the *japa* continues without a break, spontaneously. This is called unbroken meditation.

Glory of *Naam Japa*

The name of God has glory that cannot be described in words. The scriptures say that *naam japa* rewards the devotee with love and devotion to God, in addition to liberation or *moksha*. The chanting of the divine name also washes away the sins of several lifetimes. Some scholars undervalue the efficacy of the divine name and regard *naam japa* as an inferior method meant for those who are unable to practice supposedly 'superior' spiritual practices.

The glory of the divine name is underestimated because the process appears too easy. It is said in the *Bhagavata Purana* that the Lord is not different from His name and that the name is His sound incarnation. The *Puranas* declare the names of God to be the only means of salvation for Kaliyuga, thereby reducing all other spiritual practices to mere adjunctions.

In Hinduism, each deity has its own name. In fact, each deity has many names based on different aspects of manifestation. Thus, the number of names used for *japa* is quite big. One must not assume that the names that have been handed down by tradition are alone sacred and the other names cannot be chosen for *japa*.

In the endless manifestation of the glory of the Divine, there are many truths that emerge continually. All names of God are alike. Success and grace can be obtained by chanting any name with faith. Sorrow and frustration enter the minds of those who forget God. The best way to remember God is to chant His name always and under all circumstances, as Sant Tukaram has put it...

"He who utters the name of God while walking
gets the merit of sacrifice at every step.
His body becomes a place of pilgrimage.
He who repeats God's name while working
always finds perfect peace.
He who utters the name of God while eating
gets the merit of a fast
even though he has taken his meals."

Significance of Performing a Havan

Havan, a.k.a. *homam, yagna* or *yagya,* is an external form of worship. For this, an altar is built and a sacred fire is kindled using specific types of grass or wood. Oblations such as *ghee* or clarified butter, food, grains and sesame seeds are poured into the fire, while chanting mantras from the Vedas. Mantras are chanted while performing *havan* to invoke the gods and seek their blessings and favors. It is also done to ensure fulfilment of specific desires and the overall welfare of an individual, a group of people, society, nation, and the entire universe.

Historical and Mythological Perspective of *Havan*

It is believed that, during the early Vedic period, *havan* was the only ritualistic worship of God. *Puja* rituals were developed much later. The physical or the outer aspect of it was always viewed with suspicion by the followers of *gyan marg* or the path of wisdom. In *Satapatha Brahmana,* which describes the Vedic ritual associated with the *Shukla Yajurveda,* we are told that both the gods and demons tried to derive benefits by performing the *yagna.* However, the demons performed it only externally, whereas the gods also kindled the fire within them, thereby becoming immortal.

Symbolic Meaning of the Fire Ritual

One notable thing about *havan* or *yagna* is that the visible fire that you see is not worshiped. It is only a symbolic act, which is distinct from the purpose of performing the *havan*. The mantras chanted during the *havan* makes this clear:

"Oh resplendent glory, light of the universe, we light this fire and remove darkness from our midst. Similarly, by concentration and meditation, we illuminate our mind. Though dwelleth within our hearts, may we burn out all our sins and vices. Bless us Oh Lord, with kindness and generosity, knowledge and strength, food and wealth and good children and useful animals. Oh Almighty Lord, in thy name we offer all these ingredients into this sacred fire. This fire does not keep within it what it receives, but transforms everything into beneficial elements. Similarly Oh Lord, whatever we have received from thee – food and wealth, happiness and prestige, are not ours – they are thine. We place them at thy feet. We shall only keep the bare quantity with us, which is necessary for our subsistence. Let not our education, strength and wealth, make us arrogant and conceited, for they are all thine. Give us Oh Lord, such intelligence, as desired by our ancestors and learned ones."

The above translation of the prayer helps us understand the symbolic significance of fire sacrifice during the *havan*.

The Benefits of *Havan*

Havan provides the opportunity to purify the air by the removal of disease causing elements such as insects. The heat generated during a *havan* is believed to purify the surroundings and the spots where *havan* is performed is considered sanctified. The sound waves created by chanting Vedic hymns during the *havan* can purify the mind.

Idannamama chanted at the end of every mantra during a *havan* literally means 'that this is not mine; it belongs to the whole society'. It is believed that the places where a *havan* is performed is removed of sins and the people who participate in the *havan* become psychologically elevated. A *havan* also exerts a special power on women, infants and children.

๛ ॐ ๛

VI

Celebrations of Life

Why we should participate in festivals and holidays as social beings

The Significance of Shivaratri

Maha Shivratri, the night of the worship of Lord Shiva, occurs on the 14th night of the new moon during the dark half of the month of Phalguna. It falls on a moonless February night, when Hindus offer special prayer to the lord of destruction. Shivratri (In Sanskrit, 'ratri' = night) is the night when he is said to have performed the Tandava Nritya-- the dance of primordial creation, preservation and destruction. The festival is observed for one day and one night only.

Shivratri is considered especially auspicious for women. Married women pray for the well-being of their husbands and sons, while unmarried women pray for an ideal husband like Shiva, who is the spouse of Kali, Parvati and Durga.

But generally, it is believed that anyone who utters the name of Shiva during Shivratri with pure devotion is freed from all sins. He or she reaches the abode of Shiva and is liberated from the cycle of birth and death.

There are three reasons to celebrate Shivaratri:

1.   The absolute formless God, Sadashiva, appeared in the form of Lingodbhav Moorti, exactly at midnight on Shivaratri. That is why all Shiva devotees keep vigil during the night of Shivaratri and perform *Shivalinga abhishekham* at midnight. Also remember that God in his manifestation as Vishnu made his appearance as Krishna in Gokul at midnight, exactly 180 days after Shivaratri. This day is known as Janmashtami. Thus, the circle of one year (360 days) is divided into two by these two auspicious days.

2. Lord Shiva was married to Devi Parvati on Shivaratri. Shiva minus Parvati is pure *Nirgun Brahman*. With his illusive power (*maya*), Shiva becomes *Sagun Brahman* for the sake of the pious devotion of his devotees.

3. It is also believed that on Shivaratri (different *kalpa*), Lord Shiva became Neelkantham by swallowing deadly poison that emerged during the churning of the Kshira Sagar (ocean). The poison was so deadly that even a drop in His stomach, which represents the universe, would have annihilated the entire world. Hence, He held it in His neck, which turned blue due to the effect of the poison. Shivaratri is, therefore, also a day of thanksgiving to the Lord for protecting us from annihilation. The 14th shloka of *Shivmahimna Stotra* says: "O three eyed Lord, when poison came up through the churning of the ocean by the gods and demons, they were all aghast with fear as if the untimely end of all creation was imminent. In your kindness, you drank all poison, which still makes your throat blue. O Lord, even this blue mark does but increase your glory. What is apparently a blemish becomes an ornament by your intent of ridding the world of fear."

All through the day, the devotees keep severe fast, chant the sacred Panchakshara mantra "Om Namah Shivaya", and make offerings of flowers and incense to the Lord amidst ringing of temple bells. They maintain long vigils during the night, keeping awake to listen to stories, hymns and songs. The fast is broken only the next morning, after the nightlong worship. In Kashmir, the festival is held for 15 days. The 13th day is observed as a day of fast followed by a family feast.

What's Behind Holi, the Festival of Colors?

Holi or Phagwah is the most colorful festival celebrated by the followers of the Vedic religion. It is celebrated as a harvest festival and a festival to welcome the spring season.

What is Phagwah?

The word 'Phagwah' is derived from the name of the Hindu month Phalgun, because Holi is celebrated on a full moon day in the month of Phalgun. The month of Phalgun ushers in spring; this is the season when seeds sprout, flowers bloom and the country rises from winter's slumber.

Meaning of 'Holi'

'Holi' comes from the word *'hola'*, which means 'to offer oblation or prayer to the Almighty as thanksgiving for a good harvest'. Holi is celebrated every year to remind people that those who love God shall be saved and those who torture the devotees of God shall be reduced to ashes.

The Legend of Holika

Holi is also associated with the Puranic story of Holika, the sister of demon-king Hiranyakashipu. The demon-king punished his son Prahlad in a variety of ways to denounce Lord Narayana. But he failed in all his attempts. Finally, he asked his sister Holika to take Prahlad in her lap and enter a blazing fire. Holika did her brother's bidding. She had a boon that she would remain unburned even inside a fire. However, Holika's boon ended by her sinful act and she was burnt to ashes. But Prahlad came out unscathed.

The Krishna Connection

Holi is also associated with the divine dance Raaslila staged by Lord Krishna for the benefit of his devotees of Vrindavan, commonly known as the *gopis*.

The Colors of Unity and Brotherhood

Whatever is the origin of Holi or Phagwah, it has traditionally been celebrated in high spirit without any distinction of caste, creed, color, race, status or sex with the sprinkling of colored powder (*gulal*) or colored water on each other. This festival breaks all barriers of discrimination. Everyone looks the same and universal brotherhood is reaffirmed.

Navaratri: The Nine Divine Nights

'Navaratri' literally means 'nine nights.' Hindus observe this festival twice a year, once at the beginning of summer (*Vasanteeya Navaraatra*), and again at the onset of winter (*Shaardeeya Navaraatra*).

During Navaratri, the followers of Hinduism invoke the energy aspect of God in the form of the universal mother, commonly referred to as Durga, which literally means 'the remover of the miseries of life.' Durga is also referred to as Devi (goddess) or Shakti (energy or power). It is this energy that helps God proceed with the work of creation, preservation, and destruction. The worship of Shakti in a sense conforms to the scientific theory that energy is imperishable. It cannot be created or destroyed. It is always present.

Why do Hindus worship the Universal Mother?

The Hindus believe energy is only a form of the Universal Mother, who is the mother of all. We are all her children and just as children find all virtues in their mother, similarly, all of us look up to the motherhood aspect of God. In fact, Hinduism gives immense importance to the motherly side of God because we believe that mother is the creative aspect of the Absolute.

Why is Navaratri Celebrated Twice a Year?

Every year, the beginning of summer and the beginning of winter are two very important junctures of climatic change and solar influence. These two junctions have been chosen as the sacred opportunities for the worship of the divine power because:

1. Hindus believe that it is divine power that provides energy for the Earth to move around the Sun, causing the changes in the outer nature and that this divine power must be thanked for maintaining the correct balance of the universe.

2. Due to the changes in the nature, the bodies and minds of people undergo a considerable change, and hence, we worship the divine power to bestow upon all of us enough potent powers to maintain our physical and mental balance.

Why Nine Nights and Days?

Navaratri is divided into sets of three days to adore and worship different aspects of the Universal Mother. On the first three days, the Mother is invoked as a powerful force called Durga to destroy all impurities, vices and defects. On the next three days, the Mother is adored as a giver of spiritual wealth or Lakshmi, who is considered to have the power of bestowing upon her devotees inexhaustible wealth. The final three days are spent in worshipping the Mother as the Goddess of Wisdom, Saraswati. In order to have all-round success in life, we need the blessings of all the three aspects of the Universal Mother. Hence, Navratri is celebrated for nine nights.

Why Do We Need Divine Power?

Everyone in this world worships power because there is no one who does not love and long for power in some form or the other. Worshipping the Universal Mother during Navaratri is believed to bestow upon us the potent powers to cross every hurdle in life.

Ten Reasons to Celebrate Diwali

Why do we celebrate Diwali, the festival of lights? It's not just the festive mood in the air that makes you happy. It is not just that it's a good time to enjoy before the advent of winter. There are ten mythical and historical reasons why Diwali is a great time to celebrate. And there are good reasons not just for the Hindus but also for people of other religions to celebrate this great festival of lights.

1. Goddess Lakshmi's birthday: The Goddess of Wealth, Lakshmi incarnated on the new moon day (*amaavasyaa*) in the Kartik month during the churning of the ocean (*samudra manthan*). Hence Diwali is associated with Lakshmi.

2. Vishnu rescued Lakshmi: On this very day, Lord Vishnu, in his fifth incarnation (Vamana *avatar)* rescued Lakshmi from the prison of King Bali. This is another reason to worship Ma Lakshmi on Diwali.

3. Krishna killed Narakasura: On the day preceding Diwali, Lord Krishna killed the demon king Narakasura and rescued 16,000 women from his captivity. The celebration of freedom and victory went on for two days, including the Diwali day.

4. The return of the Pandavas: According to the great epic Mahabharata, it was *Kartik Amavasya* when the Pandavas appeared from their twelve years of banishment as a result of their defeat in the hands of the Kauravas in a game of dice (gambling). The subjects who loved the Pandavas celebrated the day by lighting earthen lamps.

5. The victory of Rama: According to the epic Ramayana, it was a new moon day in the Kartik month when Lord Ram, Ma Sita and Lakshmana returned to Ayodhya after vanquishing Ravana and conquering Lanka. The citizens of Ayodhya decorated the entire city with earthen lamps and illuminated the place like never before.

6. Coronation of Vikramaditya: One of the greatest Hindu Kings, Vikramaditya was coronated on Diwali day. Hence, Diwali became a historical event as well.

7. Special day for the Arya Samaj: It was on the new moon day of the Kartik month (Diwali day) when Maharishi Dayananda, one of the greatest reformers of Hinduism and the founder of Arya Samaj, attained *nirvana*.

8. Special day for the Jains: Mahavira Tirthankar, considered the founder of modern Jainism, also attained *nirvana* on Diwali day.

9. Special day for the Sikhs: The third Sikh Guru, Amar Das, institutionalized Diwali as a special day when all Sikhs gathered to receive the guru's blessings. In 1577, the foundation stone of the Golden Temple in Amritsar was laid on Diwali. In 1619, the sixth Sikh Guru Hargobind, who was held by the Mughal Emperor Jahengir, was released from the Gwalior Fort along with fifty-two kings.

10. The Pope's Diwali speech: In 1999, Pope John Paul II performed a special Eucharist in an Indian church; the altar was decorated with Diwali lamps. The Pope had a 'tilak' marked on his forehead and his speech bristled with references to the festival of light.

A Spiritual and Scientific View of Fasting

There are many auspicious occasions when fasts are observed by Hindus. They include Janmashtami, Ganesh Chaturthi, Mahashivratri, the two Navaratris, each of nine days, Ekadasi, and Pradosha. Fasting is popular not only in Hinduism, but also in Christianity, Islam, and Jainism. Fasting not only helps in yoga and spiritual attainment, but it also performs a special role in keeping the body free from diseases.

Part of Religious Ceremonies

Ancient rishis engaged in a deep thought process to understand what should be done to keep the body healthy and disease-free. They concluded that occasional rest to the digestive system is very essential to keep the body healthy. But they realized that people would not easily volunteer to miss meals, as they were addicted to food. The Hindu rishis had learnt the benefits of fasting. They knew that during a fast the body starts ejaculating harmful substances, which are responsible for causing diseases, thus keeping the body and mind in a healthy and cheerful state. Rishis also observed that fasting purified the body and soul and enhanced one's willpower immensely. Fasting also gives a tremendous impetus to devotion, faith and concentration, which are the main pillars of spiritual advancement. Therefore, the rishis, with great foresight, introduced the concept of occasional fasting during religious ceremonies.

The Body is Like a Machine

Growth of the fast food industry is a big cause of disease and ill health. Undesirable food habits are more responsible for the deterioration of health. Overeating is a major cause of lifestyle diseases that cannot be cured by drugs. At best, one can only suppress lifestyle diseases to an extent with drugs, which soon emerge in one form or the other in a more serious and severe manner. These days, people die more out of wrong eating habits than starvation.

Therefore, it is not a bad idea to keep good health by taking a break from the wrong kind of eating or overeating. Fasting is good for keeping good health. It is a natural treatment by which one can keep oneself immune from various diseases. Our body is like a machine; all the organs work like the parts of a machine. Many people give rest to all parts of the body except the digestive system. The digestive system works for twenty-four hours a day, even when we are sleeping. But if we want our bodies to work properly, then the body parts must be given proper attention and rest.

Types of Fasts

There are broadly three types of fasts:

1. **Nirahaar** – remain without food

2. **Phalalahaar** – practice a fruit-only diet

3. **Dugdhahaar** – have only cow's milk

These fasts are observed differently by different religious observers. *Nirahaar* (without food) is the best type of fasting. This can be done in two ways: *sajal* (with water) and *nirjal* (without water). In *nirjal*, even water is not taken. In *sajal* fast, lukewarm water with some lemon juice can be taken. Tea and coffee cannot be consumed in *sajal* fast.

In *phalalahaar*, only fruits and fruit juices are taken. Apple, grape and papaya are the best foods in this kind of fasting.

In *dugdhahaar*, one can take 250-500 ml of cow's milk without cream (lack of cream is very important), four to five times a day. Cow's milk is the best food; nothing is superior to cow's milk to strengthen the body. Again, tea and coffee are not permitted in *dugdhahaar*.

Breaking a Fast

People go on fasts, but they do not know how to break a fast.

Thus, they remain deprived of the utmost benefits of the fast. This is seen in local temples, where people eat plenty of rice, *roti* and other starchy foods as *mahaprasadam*, after they break the Janmashtami fast at midnight or soon after to celebrate Lord Krishna's birth. Nothing can be more harmful to the body than this kind of eating. Any type of cereal food or milk products must be avoided for at least twelve hours after breaking the fast.

A word of caution: Pregnant women and patients with high blood pressure, ulcers and diabetes should observe a fast only if their doctors have permitted them to do so.

About the Authors

Gyan Rajhans is a health and safety professional based in Canada. He has been broadcasting the only non-commercial Vedic religion radio program in North America since 1981, and a global webcast on bhajanawali.com since 1999.

Rajhans is a widely published author of religious and spiritual books, which includes a translation of the *Bhagavad Gita* in English for the younger generation. He has been conferred with various honors, including the titles of 'Rishi' by the Hindu Prarthana Samaj of Toronto, and 'Hindu Ratna' by the Hindu Federation of Canada.

Rajhans has been presenting discourses on prayer and meditation every Sunday in various Hindu Temples of the Greater Toronto Area since 1984. He received the Canadian Journalists' and Writers' Club (CEJWC) award for 2005 for his spirituality columns in South Asian Outlook e-Monthly, southasianoutlook. com.

☙ ॐ ❧

Subhamoy Das is widely known as India's first professional blogger. Since 1999, he has been writing on Hinduism in his blog on About.com, formerly part of the New York Times Company, and one of the most popular online destinations for Hinduism. His blog first appeared on the MovableType platform in 2004, transitioning into WordPress with more than a thousand posts in 2015.

Das has several years of experience as a journalist with India's leading media companies such as Hindustan Times, India Today Group, and Cybermedia India. He has authored a bestseller book on English literature for postgraduate Indian students, and five books on Indian culture and Hindu tradition for children.

With two decades of experience in media, marketing, and corporate communications, Das has worked for top multinational companies as an industry expert in B2B marketing, public relations, digital and social media, and current leads marketing and communications for a global corporation in India.

About Indus Source Books

Indus Source Books is a niche, independent book publisher in Mumbai passionately committed to publishing good and relevant literature. We believe that books are one of the most important mediums of communication and we seek to bring out publications that help to serve the community and the world we live in.

At Indus Source Books, we celebrate the diverse spiritual traditions, culture, and history of the world and present it to our readers in a contemporary format that retains its essential flavour: "Indian Spirit, Universal Wisdom".

Use the QR code below to visit our website www.indussource. com for more details.

Indus Source Books
PO Box 6194
Malabar Hill PO
Mumbai 400006
India
www.indussource.com
info@indussource.com